Short Bike Rides™
in New Jersey

"*Short Bike Rides in New Jersey* is a collection of 32 bike tours, none longer than 28 miles. . . . Mr. Santelli has also provided cultural and sightseeing information. Included are tours of varying difficulty, maps, as well as equipment and safety information."
—*New York Times*

"The tours are divided among five regions . . . and each includes a basic tour description, tips, and maps."
—*Mid-Atlantic Country*

"Santelli's style incorporates straight information about bike routes with anecdotes and other tidbits."
—*Asbury Park Press*

"There are easy to read sketch maps accompanying each suggested route, and comprehensive directions."
—*Pike County* (PA) *Dispatch*

Other Books by Robert Santelli

Aquarius Rising: The Rock Festival Years

The Big Beat: Conversations with Rock's Great Drummers,
co-authored with Max Weinberg

Sixties Rock: A Listener's Guide

Guide to the Jersey Shore

The Big Book of Blues

Short Bike Rides™ in New Jersey

Third Edition

by Robert Santelli

An East Woods Book

The Globe Pequot Press

Old Saybrook, Connecticut

Short Bike Rides is a trademark of The Globe Pequot Press, Inc.

Copyright © 1988, 1992, 1995 by Robert Santelli

Library of Congress Cataloging-in-Publication Data

Santelli, Robert.
  Short bike rides in New Jersey/by Robert Santelli.—3rd ed.
        p.   cm.
  "An East Woods book."
  ISBN 1-56440-529-X
      1. Bicycle touring—New Jersey—Guidebooks. 2. New Jersey—
  Guidebooks. I. Title.
  GV1045.5.N5S26 1995
  796.6'4'09749—dc20
                                                    95-3427
                                                    CIP

♻ This text is printed on recycled paper
Manufactured in the United States of America
Third Edition/Third Printing

For Jenna

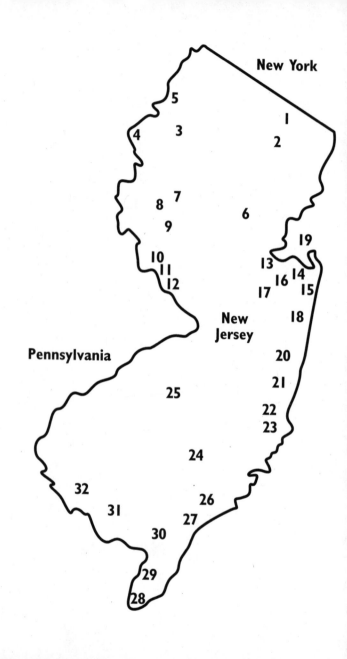

Contents

Acknowledgments

This book could not have been written without the generous help and support of William Feldman, Bicycle Advocate, New Jersey Department of Transportation; Eileen Thornton, New Jersey Department of Commerce and Economic Development, Division of Travel and Tourism; the New Jersey Bicycle Council; Steve Oliphant and the Bicycle Touring Club of North Jersey; Sandy Choron; Ann Sorrell; Dorothea Kraft; Sally McMillan, Donna Carey, Kate Siegel Bandos, Kevin Lynch, Bruce Markot, Laura Strom, E. Mace Lewis, and Linda Kennedy of The Globe Pequot Press; Kathy Micalove; Hunterdon County Park System; Pro-Tour Cycles of Westfield; and my daughters, Jaron and Jenna, and my son, Jake.

A special thanks is due my wife and partner, Cindy, who spent many hours drawing up the maps to my bike tours when she could have been happily paging through mail-order catalogues. Finally, a warm, extra-special thanks goes to Wayne Hartman, my mentor and close friend. His advice, encouragement, and love mean much to me. His influence can be found on every page of this book.

Introduction

Bicycling has been a part of my life for as long as I can remember. When I was a kid, my ten-speed was always more than a means to get me downtown or to the park. It was my first real symbol of freedom. It allowed me to explore the town I lived in as well as those communities that surrounded it. My bike gave me the chance to be on my own whenever I rode it. It also translated into responsibility and, in general, growing up.

As a teen, despite getting my driver's license and a car to commute to college, I continued to rely on my bicycle as a main means of transportation and exploration. After college, I toured Europe on a bike I bought in London, and from then on I knew intimately the immense rewards of bicycle touring. I have since bicycled throughout much of the United States and parts of Central America, Iceland, and Canada on my Claud Butler. As a journalist, I have written much about my travels and the art of bicycle touring. Today, it's a rare trip I take that doesn't include my bike.

But when I told my bicycling buddies of my plans to compile a book of bicycle tours in New Jersey, they were surprised. Why, they asked, would I want to write about bicycling in New Jersey when there were so many other places to map and describe in a bicycle tourbook?

My answer to them was twofold. I chose New Jersey because it is my home and because I've cycled in just about every region of it. I told them that writing a book such as *Short Bike Rides in New Jersey* was a way of accumulating all things pleasant that I've seen, felt, and experienced on Jersey roads into one tidy volume. In a way, I saw the book as a payback of sorts for all those memorable miles and the many more, I hope, that are in store for me and my family in the future.

The second part of my answer was less nostalgic and less personal. And it certainly was more surprising to my cycling friends than the first part of the answer. New Jersey, I said, is a fine state to tour and explore on a bicycle. I meant it. True, it has many cities and many citylike suburbs, few of which lend themselves to bicycle touring. But New Jersey also has the Shore, the mountains, the Pine Barrens, farmlands, forests, gently rolling hills, lazy country roads, and a state park system ideally suited for cycling. And the best thing about all of these is their accessibility. You don't have to travel that far to get to Cape May, for instance, even if you do live in northern New Jersey or New York.

The main focus of this book is *short* bike rides. There are important reasons why I've not included any tours exceeding thirty miles. Other bicyclists have authored books on bicycle touring in New Jersey. But virtually all of these books comprise longer, more extensive tours, aimed primarily at the more qualified cyclist who can accomplish fifty or sixty miles in one day and who can keep a steady pace from start to finish.

Short Bike Rides in New Jersey was written with the less zealous, weekend bicycle rider in mind. Every ride ends in the spot where it began, even if the ride is not exactly in the form of a loop. Most can be completed in one to two hours, although I suggest you take your time and truly enjoy the tours. Each ride includes a number of sights to see and things to do along the way. A half or full day's worth of activities and fun can be built around nearly every tour.

Short Bike Rides in New Jersey was also written with the hope of reaching as many touring cyclists as possible in this state and neighboring ones. I tried to keep in mind the needs and expectations of young cyclists and their older counterparts, novices as well as veteran riders. Members of bicycle touring clubs should also find this book useful.

Few cyclists who are in fair physical shape will find the tours contained in this book too difficult or too demanding to complete. Yet there is just enough challenge built into nearly all of them for you to know at the end of the day that your body got some exercise and stimulation.

Some tours are more strenuous than others. Less confident cyclists might wish to select those tours for which the terrain is labeled "flat" and the total mileage is less than ten. Those cyclists looking for more variety in terrain and greater challenge might prefer the tours that include hills and more substantial mileage.

If there is a theme to *Short Bike Rides in New Jersey,* it is for the reader/cyclist to see the state and as many natural, man-made, and historical treasures as possible. I am convinced that the best way to experience any area is on bicycle. The thousands of miles I've logged in more than fifteen years of touring have taught me the value of pedaling to a destination instead of driving to it. If you complete every tour in this book, you will have seen much of what is special about New Jersey. You will also become an experienced bicycle tourist, capable of longer, more challenging rides in the future.

I tried to include tours from all parts of the state in *Short Bike Rides.* There are, however, certain urban counties such as Hudson, Union, and Essex that are so densely populated and have roads so heavy with traffic that such a goal was impossible to achieve. Be forewarned, however. Not every tour in *Short Bike Rides* consists of traffic-free roads. That, too, was an impossible goal to accomplish. New Jersey is a small state; it ranks near the bottom in total square miles. And even though 40 percent of New Jersey is forestland, it still is the most densely populated state in the union.

Thus, one should obey all traffic laws when cycling, should adhere to the safety guidelines presented in "The Basics of Bicycle Touring" section, which follows this Introduction, and should always ride with caution.

There are few tours for southwestern New Jersey. Although the area has many good cycling roads, is sparsely populated, and undoubtedly possesses its share of natural beauty, there were few good routs around which to design short bike tours if I remained true to my original intentions: create rides that have a number of things to do and see along the way.

I also tried to devise unique tours to already-discovered New Jersey bicycling areas. I strove to find new roads around familiar attractions. I believe I succeeded. Where I did not, I used parts of existing tours that were available to me and that met the general guidelines of this book. Where entire tours were used, credit has been given to the appropriate bicycle club or government agency.

Every effort has been made to ensure accuracy of both the directions and the maps of each tour. I rode every tour in the book twice:

3

once on my bicycle and once in a car. Cindy Kraft, my illustrator (also my wife), participated the second time around. We tried to make the maps and the words that embellish them as simple and as straightforward as possible. Only you, the touring cyclist, will know if we did a good job.

Bicycle touring can be enjoyed almost any time of the year in New Jersey. Spring, summer, and fall are certainly better than winter for obvious reasons. The best time to complete the bike tours near or at the Shore would be, of course, summer. But don't discount fall, especially September, since there is much less traffic on Shore roads then, and you still have air and water temperatures warm enough for a dip in the ocean.

Spring and fall are fine seasons to complete the other tours, although Jersey springs are apt to be wet. Experience has taught me that fall is the best time to get out and experience New Jersey on your bike. If possible, ride the tours in north, northwest, and western New Jersey in late September, October, or early November. It is then that the trees are awash in color. Such a spectacle will make your ride that much more rewarding and memorable.

Finally, a few words about how to use this book: Read through the directions to each tour and become familiar with the maps before you begin. You will save a lot of "stop and go" time. Then, out on the road, refer to the simplified set of directions included with each tour.

It's also a good idea to bring along an up-to-date county map. I am fond of *Hagstrom* maps; they're usually available in better stationery stores and bookshops. Even though *Short Bike Rides in New Jersey* has been carefully researched, roads might have since closed for paving or other construction, side streets that were two-way might now be one-way, and stop signs might have given way to traffic lights. There really is no way for a bicycle guidebook writer to protect against these changes except to note them and make the necessary alterations in the book's next edition—which is what I have done here. If you come across any such aberrations or detours, refer to the county map to get you back on track.

I also recommend that you have a quality handlebar pannier, preferably with a see-through plastic shield under which maps and

4

books like this one may be kept. A simple glance at the map and directions from time to time will be all you need if you follow my advice and become familiar with your chosen tour prior to setting out. And whenever the directions and map are more comprehensive and dictate a more careful, detailed look, having the book close at hand is more convenient than searching through a stuffed backpack or rear pannier.

Enough said. Now it's time to tour. Select one ride that tickles your fancy and be off. Hopefully, you'll have as much fun completing the tours in this book as I did researching, riding, and ultimately writing about them.

Happy cycling.

The Basics of Bicycle Touring

Bicycle touring requires more than a bike and scenic roads. You need to do some advanced planning. You need the right kinds of equipment and clothing to make your tour, no matter what the distance or difficulty, a pleasant one. By reading through this book and selecting a tour, you've already begun the preparation stage.

Carefully read through the tour you choose at least twice. Take into account the mileage, the region of New Jersey it passes through, the terrain, and the attractions along the way. Be certain it is a tour you will be able to complete—and enjoy.

The second part of the preparation stage is making sure your bike is road-ready. The easiest way to spoil a day on the road, aside from bad weather or excess traffic, is a mechanical breakdown. Eliminate the potential for broken spokes, malfunctioning brakes and derailleurs, and flat tires by having a reputable bicycle mechanic check over your bike before you depart. No one, of course, can guarantee every tour to be hassle-free, but a thorough tune-up should minimize bicycle breakdowns.

Most bicycle tourists who never venture off the road need only a standard ten-speed bike to complete the tours in this book. Although mountain or all-terrain bikes are popular, they are unnecessary for the kind of touring outlined in *Short Bike Rides*. The best mountain bikes are rugged machines, specifically suited for terrains other than smooth road surfaces, although you can certainly use a mountain bike, if that's what you own, to complete any tour in this book.

(*Note:* There is one tour in which a mountain bike is preferred over a traditional ten-speed. That tour is the one in the Edwin B. Forsythe National Wildlife Refuge. It has a rough, gravel surface, perhaps a problem for ten-speeds and their skinny tires, but a cinch for mountain bikes and their wider, knobbed tires. A few other tours have some stretches where the cyclist must proceed with caution due to a rough road surface.)

Most experienced cyclists know that toe clips (or toe straps), those funny-looking foot cages attached to the pedals, make the pedalling process more efficient. The energy spent getting from one point to another on a bicycle taxes your leg muscles. It makes sense, then, to spread the pedaling task over as many leg muscles as possible. Riding with toe clips will help you become a better bicycle rider and cut down on leg fatigue when touring.

Fenders are also a good idea. You'll appreciate them most when the roads are wet. Fenders will keep you drier and cleaner. If you don't pretend to be a bike racer when touring, the extra weight of front and rear fenders is so small that it will not trouble you.

Water bottles are a must for obvious reasons. Two are better than one, especially during warm weather. Keep one bottle in the water bottle bracket attached to your bike frame. Keep the other in your saddlebag or pannier.

You will need something to carry a camera, some snacks, sunglasses, and other personal items. A front handlebar pannier should suffice. You can store maps and this book in a waterproof pannier with a see-through plastic shield. There are many panniers and packs on the market. Be choosey.

So much for tour planning and bicycle preparation. What about equipment to bring with you on the road? You certainly don't want a bike loaded down with unnecessary gear. Travel light. There are few essentials, however, that you will be glad you brought along should something go wrong.

A toolbag and some basic tools are a must. Bring what you think you might need. Certainly an adjustable crescent wrench (4-inch or 6-inch), a small pliers, an Allen wrench set, a screwdriver, and at least two tire irons are mandatory. So is a tire patch kit. And don't forget a pocketknife and a compact, easy-to-use bicycle repair book. A spoke wrench, a freewheel tool, and a chain tool are wise to bring if you know how to use them. Also in the toolbag might be an extra brake cable (rear), six extra spokes. an extra brake pad, and a spare tire tube.

If you get a flat, you'll be glad you brought along an air pump that works. If you misjudge dusk and darkness, a small portable light will come in handy. A lock and cable are a necessity if you plan to leave your bike for any period of time. A safety flag enables cars to see you and adjust their speed and road position.

Fashion has become a big part of the bicycle clothing industry lately. Bicyclists want to look good on the road. There is nothing wrong with that; however, there is something wrong when fashion becomes the only point of comparison when selecting a riding outfit. A bicycle tourist can accomplish any tour in this book wearing a pair of jeans or shorts, a pair of sneakers, a shirt, and, depending on the weather, a jacket or sweatshirt. But if you plan to take bicycle touring seriously and hope to ride fairly often, it is smart to invest in a few garments that will surely make your ride more comfortable.

A good pair of cycling shorts, for instance, is a wise investment. Select a pair with a chamois-lined crotch to absorb sweat. Also, make certain the shorts are long enough to prevent chafing on your inner thighs. Cotton, wool, or polypropylene are better than nylon or polyester shorts.

Another good investment is a pair of cycling shoes. If you only stick to the type of tours in this book, you will not be doing any extensive, long-distance riding. Select a shoe that is lightweight and comfortable, yet thick-soled. You'll be making stops along the way to visit museums and other attractions, so stay away from cleated shoes. They are almost impossible to walk in comfortably. You want versatility in your cycling shoes—you will need to walk as well as ride in them.

Bold, bright-colored cycling shirts are very popular—and a good idea. A driver is more apt to spot you on the road if you wear bright clothing while touring. These shirts, though, are usually expensive. Cyclists not ready to shell out sixty dollars or so might look for a simple, yet colorful, cotton shirt. A long-sleeved shirt is a good idea for early morning rides. Thin layers of clothing are always better than bulk; they keep you warmer and may be removed individually if necessary.

A lightweight, easy-to-stuff windbreaker, preferably one made of Gore-Tex, is another sound investment. There are many cheap windbreakers on the market—you get what you pay for. Don't skimp here. A quality Gore-Tex windbreaker is waterproof, yet it allows air to circulate so you don't become soaked with perspiration. You can use such a windbreaker not only for cycling but for other outdoor activities too. The only drawback to a Gore-Tex windbreaker: the price. A good one may cost a hundred dollars or more.

Forget about those cute cycling caps bicycle racers wear. Do yourself a favor and opt for a helmet. Buy the best one you can afford. Your helmet could save your life. Find out how well the helmet you select will protect your head in a serious spill. Ask questions about its design and get answers before you reach for your wallet.

It pays to do a bit of research on what constitutes a quality helmet. Once again, there are lots of helmets on the market. Check the consumer section of the bicycling magazines found at your local newsstand or bike shop for the latest information on the newest helmets and helmet design.

Gloves with padded leather palms will help prevent your hands from hurting on longer tours. Holding onto the handlebar can get tedious and tiresome. Make sure the finger openings on the gloves you buy are not so tight that they hinder blood circulation. Cycling gloves should fit snugly.

Try to avoid riding in the rain. It's dangerous and not very rewarding. But if you do get caught in a downpour, you'll be glad you brought along a rain cape or poncho. A good alternative to a cape or poncho is your Gore-Tex windbreaker. It won't cover you like a cape, but at least the upper part of your body will stay dry while you search for shelter.

Ten Touring Tips

If you bought this book, you undoubtedly know how to ride a bicycle. But pedaling to the store or to the railroad station is a bit different from completing a thirty-mile tour of a section of New Jersey's countryside.

Here are ten touring tips to keep in mind when you ride. They will help you grow from a novice bicycle tourist into an experienced one.

1. If you ride a bike on New Jersey roads, you must obey traffic laws. *Stop* at stop signs and red traffic signals. Take a defensive position when passing through "yield" intersections, yellow traffic signals, and high traffic areas.

2. When riding in residential areas or towns, beware of pedestrians, car doors suddenly opening. and cars pulling out of driveways. On rural roads, keep a sharp eye out for dogs.

3. When riding on major thoroughfares, stay inside the shoulder area. If there isn't a designated shoulder, imagine there is one, and ride within its boundaries.

4. Always be on the lookout for rocks, broken pavement, oil slicks, wet leaves, glass, and loose gravel. Hitting any of this debris could cause you to spill or give your bike a flat tire.

5. Pace yourself and don't be afraid to take frequent rests. Bicycle touring is supposed to be fun. If you push yourself too hard, you'll miss the scenery and the serenity that touring offers the cyclist.

6. Don't wait to drink until you're thirsty. Don't wait to snack until you're hungry.

7. Use the gears on your bike efficiently. Low gears are for going up hills; high gears are for coming down. Flat terrain requires a gear in between. According to Bike Centennial, a popular bicycle touring organization, a "brisk, steady cadence of 65–80 pedal revolutions per minute" equals proficient cycling.

8. If you're touring with a companion, practice the cycling technique of drafting, especially in headwinds. Here is how it works: The lead rider cuts wind resistance for the rider(s) behind. The second rider in the draft should stay approximately one to two feet from the lead rider's rear tire. The second rider should also stay a half foot to the right of the lead rider. Communication is important when drafting. The lead rider must relay information to the rider(s) concerning traffic, turns, road debris, and other road hazards.

9. Make sure your brakes are in working order before any ride, but especially rides that contain hills. When braking, apply equal pressure to front and rear brakes.

10. Whenever you leave your bike, even if it's only for a moment, lock it. Don't forget to take your handlebar pannier with you. If you don't, its contents might not be there when you return.

Neither the author nor The Globe Pequot Press assumes any liability for accidents happening to or injuries sustained by readers who engage in the activities described in this book.

Ringwood Roundabout

County:	Passaic
Number of Miles:	11.3
Degree of Difficulty:	Moderate to difficult
Terrain:	Some hills
Surface:	Good
Things to See:	Ringwood State Park, Skylands Manor Carriage House, New Jersey Botanical Gardens, Shepherd Lake, Ringwood Manor and Museum, Wanaque Reservoir

Some years ago I was assigned by *New Jersey Monthly* magazine to rate and write a cover story about the state parks of New Jersey. It was a challenging but rewarding assignment. I had to visit all the state parks and then personally judge each of them. I took into consideration what they had to offer (activities, museums, special events, and so on) as well as general upkeep and overall beauty.

Of the twenty-five or so state parks that I visited and wrote about in the article, I rated Ringwood number one. And after returning to many of the parks to put together bike tours for this book, I found that Ringwood still rates at the top of my list or at least in the top three. (Other big favorites of mine are Island Beach and Washington Crossing. Both have bicycle tours well worth riding. See the Jersey Shore and Western New Jersey sections of this book.)

The Ringwood Roundabout tour is a hilly one, and part of it is on a major thoroughfare. There is no getting around the hills or Greenwood Lake Turnpike (Route 511), however. Thus, Ringwood Roundabout might not be a tour for the novice bicycle tourist to try first even though it appears first in this book. Complete some of the easier tours, gain some road experience, and tune up your leg muscles so

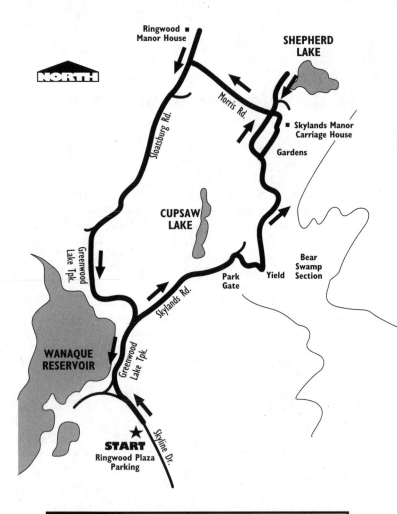

Ringwood ■
Manor House

**SHEPHERD
LAKE**

NORTH

Sloatsburg Rd.

Morris Rd.

■ **Skylands Manor
Carriage House**

Gardens

**CUPSAW
LAKE**

Greenwood Lake Tpk.

**Bear
Swamp
Section**

**Park
Gate**

Yield

Skylands Rd.

**WANAQUE
RESERVOIR**

Greenwood Lake Tpk.

★
**START
Ringwood Plaza
Parking**

Skyline Dr.

HOW
to get
there
Garden State Parkway, exit 154, to Route 46 West.
Route 46 West to Route 23 North. Route 23 North to
Route 511 North. Route 511 North to Skyline Drive in
Ringwood. Ringwood Plaza, the tour's starting point, is on
Skyline Drive.

Ringwood Roundabout: Directions at a glance

1. Left out of Ringwood Plaza and onto Skyline Drive.
2. Right onto Greenwood Lake Turnpike.
3. Right onto Skylands Road.
4. Enter Skylands Manor section of Ringwood State Park.
5. Right at first intersection in park.
6. Right at yield sign. (Enter New Jersey Botanical Gardens section of Ringwood State Park.)
7. Bear left at fork.
8. Right at stop sign. Visit Skylands Manor Carriage House and Visitor's Center and New Jersey Botanical Gardens.
9. Left out of Visitor's Center.
10. Bear right at fork.
11. Turn right at stop sign.
12. Pass through second stop sign intersection and ride to Shepherd Lake.
13. Backtrack from Shepherd Lake; bear right at fork and turn right at stop sign two hundred feet away (onto Morris Road).
14. Turn right at Morris Road/Sloatsburg Road intersection. Ride to Ringwood Manor House on Sloatsburg Road.
15. After visiting Ringwood Manor House, backtrack on Sloatsburg Road. Pass intersection with Morris Road.
16. Left at stop sign onto Greenwood Lake Turnpike.
17. Left onto Skyline Drive.
18. Right into Ringwood Plaza.

that climbing hills isn't an imposing or disagreeable task. Then Ringwood Roundabout can be enjoyed, and its many sites, both natural and historical, can be truly appreciated.

The tour begins in the Ringwood Plaza parking lot on Skyline Drive in the town of Ringwood. Exit the plaza and turn left onto Skyline Drive. A few hundred yards away, you'll come to a stop sign and a dangerous intersection. Go straight after passing the stop sign, but do so with caution. Proceed down Skyline Drive to another stop sign, this one at the Greenwood Lake Turnpike intersection. Make a right here and ride north on Greenwood Lake Turnpike. On your left is the picturesque Wanaque Reservoir. Stay as far to the right of the road as possible since the speed limit is 50 miles per hour for autos and there are no shoulders.

About two miles up the road you'll come to the turnoff for Skylands Road. Bear right onto Skylands Road and begin your climb to the south entrance of the Skylands Manor section of Ringwood State Park, located about a mile away at the top of the hill.

Enter the park. Some five hundred feet down the road you'll come to an intersection. Make a right and follow the flat, pleasant, one-way road with small ponds, fields, and trees on both sides of it. You'll find that one section of the road has trees that extend high overhead, forming a natural canopy that is striking during the fall.

You'll eventually come to a yield sign. Bear right. You'll now enter the New Jersey Botanical Gardens area of Ringwood State Park. At the next fork, bear left. (A DO NOT ENTER sign prevents you from going right.) Ride down the road to the stop sign, where you'll make a right and pedal up the hill to the Skylands Manor Carriage House and Visitor's Center, located on your left side. The Carriage House is the headquarters for the Skylands Association, a nonprofit organization that helps maintain the New Jersey Botanical Gardens, located adjacent to the Carriage House.

Visitors are permitted to stroll through the Botanical Gardens. You can pick up a free map of the gardens at the Visitor's Center and take in the sights and smells of one of Ringwood's most popular attractions. The Botanical Gardens comprise many small gardens, including a bog and wildflower garden, a lilac and azalea garden, and a magnolia walk.

Opposite the Carriage House and Visitor's Center is Skylands Manor, a 1920s mansion designed by renowned architect John Russell Pope. Skylands Manor is made of gray granite extracted from the nearby Ramapo Mountains. It has forty-five rooms, many of which are being restored. Unfortunately, Skylands Manor is open to the public on a very limited basis due to the renovation.

After your visit to the Botanical Gardens, continue down the road. Bear right at the fork and proceed through the large gates to the stop sign, where you'll turn right. A quarter mile or so down the road, you'll come to another stop sign. You might notice that you've already ridden down this road, on your way to the Botanical Gardens. Actually, you've just completed a loop. (If you turned right at this stop sign, you'd head back to the Skylands Manor Carriage House and Visitor's Center.) Proceed through the stop sign and head toward Shepherd Lake, your next destination.

There is swimming, picnicking, and boating on Shepherd Lake. But if you're in Ringwood State Park to cycle, you'll want to admire the scenery, maybe have a snack here, and ride on. Because there is no other exit out of the park, however, you must backtrack a bit to complete this tour. Ride back on the same road that took you to Shepherd Lake. At the fork, bear right and go to the stop sign, two hundred feet away.

Make a right at the stop sign. You're now on Morris Road, though there is no street sign to indicate such. Ride down one hill and up the next. Pass the Mount St. Francis Retreat Center and a small residential area. You'll notice that you are no longer in the Skylands section of Ringwood State Park. Ride to the intersection of Morris Road and Sloatsburg Road. Make a right onto Sloatsburg Road and head to Ringwood Manor House, about a mile away. Sloatsburg Road is a major thoroughfare, so ride with caution.

The Ringwood Manor House is a National Historic Landmark and the former home of such noted families as the Coopers and Hewitts. Peter Cooper was a wealthy New York philanthropist and the founder of Cooper Union institute. Abraham Hewitt was a nineteenth-century ironmaster who supplied much of the area with iron products. Inside the Manor House are relics from the iron-making days at Ringwood and collections of antiques and period pieces. Visitors can also view a deck gun from the U.S.S. *Constitution* ("Old Ironsides"), America's famous naval vessel.

After you've toured Ringwood Manor House, go back out the driveway and return to Sloatsburg Road. Make a right and head in the same direction from which you came. Pass the intersection with Morris Road where you exited the Skylands section of Ringwood State Park. Continue on Sloatsburg Road to the intersection with Greenwood Lake Turnpike a couple of miles away.

Make a left onto Greenwood Lake Turnpike. This is a major roadway, so ride with caution. On your right is the Wanaque Reservoir. Eventually you'll pass the Skylands Road intersection where you turned off to enter Ringwood State Park earlier in the tour. Continue on Greenwood Lake Turnpike until you come to the intersection with Skyline Drive. Make a left here and ride up the hill to Ringwood Plaza, the tour's starting point.

Ringwood Ramble

County:	Passaic
Number of Miles:	20
Degree of Difficulty:	Difficult
Terrain:	Some hills
Surface:	Good
Things to See:	Wanaque Reservoir, back roads of Ringwood and West Milford Township, Wanaque Wildlife Management Area

Like the Ringwood Roundabout, this tour also originates at Ringwood Plaza. Although the ride contains some hills, they are not the reason Ringwood Ramble is judged "difficult." The rating has to do with the roads. Few of them have spacious shoulders where touring cyclists can ride comfortably and without competing for roadspace with cars. Thus, the cyclist must take special caution on those tour roads where the speed limit is above thirty-five miles per hour.

Don't let this discourage you, though. This tour was built around a longer, more comprehensive tour of Ringwood and West Milford's back roads that is frequently used by the Bicycle Touring Club of North Jersey. Because of the rural nature of this part of Passaic County, almost none of the roads have the kind of wide, well-paved shoulders found in other sections of the state.

To start the tour, exit the Ringwood Plaza parking lot and make a left onto Skyline Drive. A few hundred yards away, you'll come to a stop sign and a dangerous intersection. Go straight after passing the stop sign, but do so with caution. Proceed down Skyline Drive to a second stop sign, this one at the Greenwood Lake Turnpike intersection. Make a left and ride south on Greenwood Lake Turnpike. On your right is the Wanaque Reservoir.

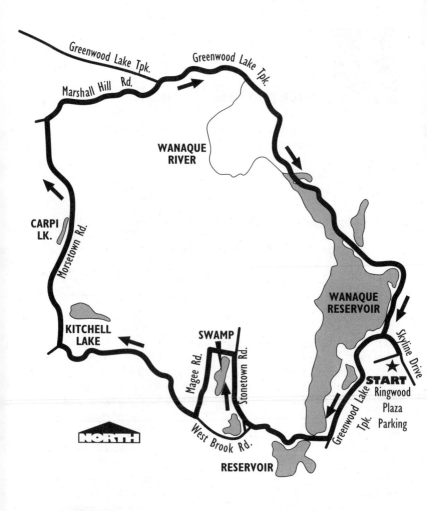

NORTH

HOW to get there — Garden State Parkway, exit 154, to Route 46 West. Route 46 West to Route 23 North. Route 23 North to Route 511 North. Route 511 North to Skyline Drive in Ringwood. Ringwood Plaza, the tour's starting point, is on Skyline Drive.

Ringwood Ramble: Directions at a Glance

1. Left out of Ringwood Plaza onto Skyline Drive.
2. Left onto Greenwood Lake Turnpike.
3. Right onto West Brook Road.
4. Bear right at "island" onto Stonetown Road.
5. Left just beyond Ringwood Boro Fire House onto Magee Road.
6. Right back onto West Brook Road.
7. Right onto Morsetown Road.
8. Right onto Marshall Hill Road, which becomes Greenwood Lake Turnpike.
9. Greenwood Lake Turnpike to Skyline Drive.
10. Left onto Skyline Drive to Ringwood Plaza.

About a mile and a half from the point where you turned onto the turnpike is West Brook Road. Make a right on West Brook. This is a snug road, and there are a few tight bends, so ride with caution. The view of the southern section of the Wanaque Reservoir is splendid.

You'll come to an "island" in the middle of West Brook Road about a mile or so later. Bear right. You'll now be on Stonetown Road. Proceed on Stonetown Road until you see the Ringwood Boro Fire House on your left. Just beyond the fire house is Magee Road. Turn left onto Magee Road.

You'll ride over a small bridge and remain on Magee Road until the "T" intersection. Make a right at the "T" back onto West Brook Road. Continue on West Brook. You'll pass Kitchell Lake on your right. Immediately after the lake is Morsetown Road. Make a right on Morsetown.

Be prepared for some hill climbing as Morsetown Road winds through the heart of West Milford Township. Up the road a bit you'll pass Capri Lake on your left and some scattered residential areas. Although Morsetown Road has no real shoulders, it is not a major road and traffic is usually light.

Continue on Morsetown Road to the "T" intersection. Here

Morsetown runs into Marshall Hill Road. Make a right and follow Marshall Hill to Greenwood Lake Turnpike. At the fork, bear right. Eventually Marshall Hill Road merges with Greenwood Lake Turnpike, also known as Route 511.

You'll remain on Greenwood Lake Turnpike until the intersection with Skyline Drive and the return to Ringwood Plaza, some seven miles later. You'll pass a portion of the Wanaque Wildlife Management Area and cross over the Wanaque River, which connects the Wanaque Reservoir and Greenwood Lake.

You'll also encounter a couple of fork intersections. Bear right at both of them and follow Route 511 signs. This is a major road; some sections of it have shoulders, but most don't. Fortunately the road is wide and you're able to stay out of the way of cars. Ride with caution, nonetheless. The speed limit on Greenwood Lake Turnpike (Route 511) is fifty miles per hour.

Eventually you'll come to a long stretch of Greenwood Lake Turnpike that hugs the northern section of the Wanaque Reservoir. Enjoy the view of the clear, blue water and the tiny islands that dot the basin.

Greenwood Lake Turnpike will gradually bend around the reservoir. The road should be familiar to those cyclists who have ridden the Ringwood Roundabout tour, once they are on the eastern shore of the Wanaque Reservoir. There is an "island" at the base of Skyline Drive with flagpoles bearing the United States and state of New Jersey flags.

Turn left here onto Skyline Drive, and ride up the steep hill back to Ringwood Plaza where the tour ends.

Swartswood Lake Loop

County:	Sussex
Number of Miles:	12
Degree of Difficulty:	Moderate
Terrain:	Some hills
Surface:	Good
Things to See:	Villages of Stillwater and Middleville, Robbins General Store, Swartswood Lake, Swartswood Lake State Park

Swartswood Lake is a popular northwest New Jersey destination for bathers and boaters. Swartswood Lake State Park isn't a large park—the lake is surely the main attraction—but the bicycle ride to and through the park is indeed worthwhile. And when the weather is hot there is always the opportunity for a cool dip in the lake.

The tour begins in the village of Stillwater at the intersection of routes 521 and 610. Located across from this intersection is the Stillwater Historical Society Building. Proceed up Route 521 North (Stillwater Road) toward the village of Middleville. Route 521 isn't a heavy traffic road, but cars will certainly pass you often enough to warrant riding with caution. Be prepared, too, for a few climbs and descents, although no hill that you'll encounter is particularly challenging.

About three miles up the road at the Middleville Inn, you'll see a sign for Route 521, Swartswood, and Branchville. Make a right. Immediately thereafter you'll come to Robbins General Store, a delightful place to stop for a snack or drink. Notice that the store is also Middleville's post office and has Middleville's one and only gas pump.

Continue along Route 521 North. About a mile after leaving Middleville you'll get your first glance of Swartswood Lake on your right.

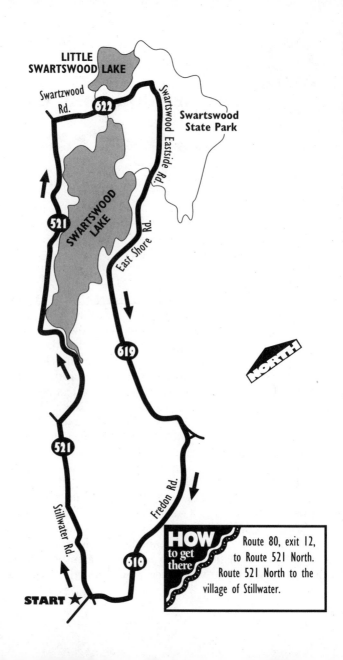

Swartswood Lake Loop: Directions at a Glance

1. Route 521 North to Middleville Inn. Make a right. (You're still on Route 521, however.)
2. Right onto Route 622.
3. Right onto Route 619.
4. Right onto Route 610.
5. Follow Route 610 to Route 610–Route 521 intersection, the tour's starting and stopping point.

What you'll see, however, is only a small, skinny finger of Swartswood. The lake gets bigger and wider up ahead.

Proceed on Route 521 North to the intersection with Route 622, also known as Swartswood Road. You'll see a sign for Swartswood State Park, too. Make a right here. A half mile down Route 622, you'll enter Swartswood Lake State Park property.

Proceed on Route 622 until the intersection with Route 619. Make a right here. (Route 619 is also known as Swartswood Eastside Road and once you leave the park, East Shore Drive. It's easiest to follow signs for Route 619.)

Approximately a half mile down Route 619 you'll come to the formal entrance of Swartswood State Park on your right. Pull into the park if only to get a good glimpse of Swartswood Lake. You can purchase food and drinks here, or, as already mentioned, you can go swimming. Some cyclists might opt for a picnic lunch and a swim—a great idea if you want to make this tour an all-day activity.

Afterwards, leave Swartswood Lake State Park the same way you came in and make a right back onto Route 619. Proceed on Route 619 to the fork intersection with Route 610 (Fredon Road), some four miles south of the Swartswood Lake State Park entrance/exit. Bear right. A hundred yards later you'll come to a stop sign. Bear right again. You'll now be on Route 610.

Follow Route 610 back into Stillwater. Along the way you'll pass

some picturesque horse farms and ride over a single-lane bridge. You'll then enter the village of Stillwater and pass the Inn at Stillwater, a couple of antiques shops, and the Old Stillwater General Store. All of this is just a hundred yards or so from the Route 610–Route 521 intersection, the starting point of the tour.

Delaware Water Gap

County:	Sussex
Number of Miles:	11.4
Degree of Difficulty:	Moderate to difficult
Terrain:	Some hills
Surface:	Good
Things to See:	Delaware Water Gap National Recreation Area, Delaware River, Walpack Wildlife Management Area

Sometimes it is difficult to believe that the Delaware Water Gap National Recreation Area is actually a part of New Jersey. The rich mountain landscapes; the cool, crisp air; the thick forests; and the abundant wildlife make the Delaware Water Gap seem far removed from New Jersey's urban bustle and congested suburbs. Incredibly, most of northern and central New Jersey's largest towns and cities, from Paterson to New Brunswick, are little more than an hour's drive from the Delaware Water Gap. Along with southern New Jersey's Pine Barrens (see The Pine Barrens tour), the Water Gap is a treasure trove of unspoiled natural beauty. And, like the Pine Barrens, it's a great place to cycle.

But what about all the ridges and steep inclines, you ask? Just how rewarding can climbing the Kittatinny Mountain Range on a bicycle be? Have no fear. Where there are rivers, there are usually valleys and some pretty good flatland. And where there is flatland in a mountainous region, there is probably a road. Such is the case here.

Actually, getting to the Delaware Water Gap tour starting point by car is considerably more challenging than riding it by bike. Although there are a couple of good bike climbs, none are so demanding that

27

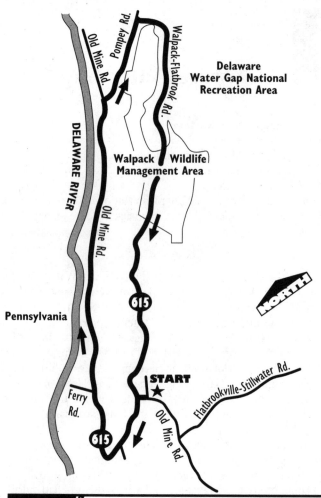

Delaware Water Gap National Recreation Area

Walpack Wildlife Management Area

Pompey Rd.

Old Mine Rd.

Walpack-Flatbrook Rd.

DELAWARE RIVER

Old Mine Rd.

Pennsylvania

615

NORTH

START

Flatbrookville-Stillwater Rd.

Ferry Rd.

Old Mine Rd.

615

HOW to get there — Route 80, exit 12, to Route 521 North. Route 521 North to Route 617. Route 617 to Route 624. Route 624 to Flatbrookville-Stillwater Road. Flatbrookville-Stillwater Road to Old Mine Road. Old Mine Road to intersection with Route 615 (Walpack-Flatbrook Road).

Delaware Water Gap: Directions at a Glance

1. Left at the stop sign where Route 615 and Old Mine Road merge.
2. Proceed on Route 615/Old Mine Road.
3. Right at the fork onto Pompey Road.
4. Right back onto Route 615.
5. Route 615 to starting/stopping point.

the tour should be judged "difficult." One section of the tour follows the Delaware River. Another section follows the Flat Brook. Both make for pleasurable riding.

It is a good idea to make certain you have adequate water, tools, and whatever snacks you might want to munch on along the way before you start out. There are no stores and few houses on the route. Traffic will probably be light, except on summer weekends. The roads are patrolled by park rangers, and there is a ranger station farther north on Route 615. Thus, if an emergency should occur, help isn't too far away.

The tour begins at the merge of Old Mine Road and Route 615 (Walpack-Flatbrook Road). Park your car in the small parking area on the side of the Old Mine Road Bridge that's usually reserved for fishermen. Facing the stop sign at the Old Mine Road–Route 615 merge, make a left and ride south on Route 615/Old Mine Road. Ride with caution; the road has no shoulders.

About a mile from your starting point, you'll pass a historical marker on the opposite side of the road. It gives a brief account of the historical importance of Old Mine Road, which allegedly was cleared and opened for travel around 1650. This would make it the oldest road still in use in the United States.

After you round the bend on Route 615/Old Mine Road, you'll begin to catch glimpses of the Delaware River on your left. Across it is Pennsylvania. As you continue north on Old Mine Road, you'll see cars parked on the sides of the road. Often these are the vehicles of bird watchers and hikers, but during hunting season they are almost always the cars of hunters. The pops you'll undoubtedly hear off in the distance are the sounds of hunters' guns.

About five miles or so from the Old Mine Road historical marker, you'll come to a fork in the road. To your left is Old Mine Road. To your right is Pompey Road. Take the latter. North of this intersection, Old Mine Road is not in good shape generally. Besides, Pompey Road offers the only Water Gap loop connection to your starting point.

Pompey Road is the steepest climb you'll encounter on this tour. At the end of it, approximately two miles away, you'll come to a stop sign and the Route 615 intersection. Make a right and head south on Route 615, also known in this section as Walpack-Flatbrook Road. Soon you'll enter the Walpack Wildlife Management Area. On your left is the Flat Brook.

Continue south on Route 615 to the Old Mine Road Bridge, your starting and ending point. In the fall this area is ablaze with color. Be advised, though, that the leaves fall off the trees earlier here than in other sections of the state. If you plan your ride sometime during the foliage spectacle, the best time to go is late September or early October.

Old Mine Road Run

County:	Warren
Number of Miles:	24
Degree of Difficulty:	Moderate
Terrain:	Some hills
Surface:	Fair
Things to See:	Delaware Water Gap National Recreation Area, Worthington State Forest, Delaware Water Gap Visitor's Center, Delaware River, Old Mine Road, Millbrook Village

The Old Mine Road Run is a sister tour of the Delaware Water Gap tour. Both are located in the Delaware Water Gap National Recreation Area. Both are particularly scenic rides along the Delaware River. But where the Delaware Water Gap tour is a loop tour that begins and ends at the same point without covering any road twice, the Old Mine Road Run is a "backtrack" tour. In other words, cyclists will ride up Old Mine Road from the Delaware Water Gap Visitor's Center to Millbrook Village, a restored, century-old Water Gap community. Then they will turn around and return to the Visitor's Center, once again, by way of Old Mine Road.

There is no other way to enjoy the scenery of Old Mine Road and end up where you started. Roads are scarce in the Water Gap Recreation Area. Those alternative roads, which a touring cyclist might consider as a way to avoid backtracking on Old Mine Road, are not always maintained or else go in the wrong direction. Any attempt at riding on these roads would require more time and a fat-tire mountain bike. The tour would also add up to much more than twenty-four miles.

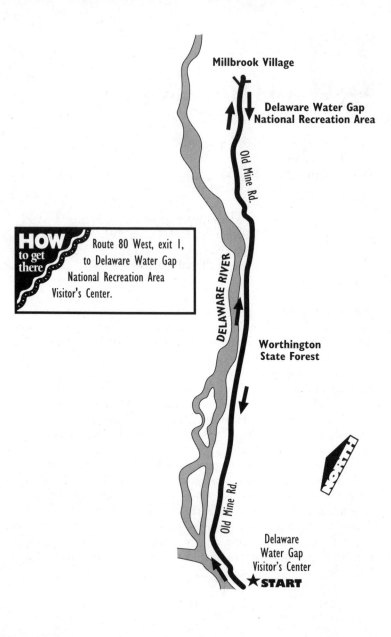

Millbrook Village

Delaware Water Gap
National Recreation Area

Old Mine Rd.

HOW to get there

Route 80 West, exit 1,
to Delaware Water Gap
National Recreation Area
Visitor's Center.

DELAWARE RIVER

Worthington
State Forest

NORTH

Old Mine Rd.

Delaware
Water Gap
Visitor's Center
★ START

Old Mine Road Run: Directions at a Glance

1. Delaware Water Gap Visitor's Center parking lot to Old Mine Road.
2. Old Mine Road to Millbrook Village.
3. Old Mine Road back to Delaware Water Gap Visitor's Center.

There is really no disadvantage to riding up and down Old Mine Road. It is one of the prettiest stretches of road in all New Jersey. Although you share the road with automobiles, bicycle traffic is common on Old Mine Road, especially on weekends in spring, summer, and fall.

As mentioned in the Delaware Water Gap tour, travelers supposedly began using Old Mine Road as early as 1650. Dutch settlers in New Jersey and New York used it to haul copper ore from the Pahaquarry Mines in New Jersey to what is today Kingston, New York. The Old Mine Road is said to be the oldest road in America still in use. Its length is more than a hundred miles.

Leave your car in the parking lot of the Delaware Water Gap Visitor's Center just off the western end (or beginning) of Route 80. Inside the Visitor's Center are free brochures and maps of the Recreation Area and a few small displays that explain the geological origins of the Delaware Water Gap millions of years ago. Rangers stationed at the Visitor's Center will answer any question you might have about the Recreation Area.

Like the Delaware Water Gap tour described earlier, the Old Mine Road Run is without stores or places to stop and eat. Bring with you what you want to snack on or drink. Also, make certain you take the proper tools and spare parts (see the bicycle touring information in the beginning of the book) with you in case a breakdown or tire puncture should occur. If there is an emergency, however, there are enough cars traveling on Old Mine Road so it would not be impossible to flag one down. Also, park rangers patrol Old Mine Road on a routine basis.

Ride out of the Visitor's Center parking lot and make a left onto the service road that leads to Old Mine Road a few hundred yards away. Not far from the Visitor's Center you'll come to, of all things, a traffic light. It's there because this section of Old Mine Road isn't wide enough for two cars to pass at the same time. A red light for you means a green light for cars heading to the Visitor's Center and Route 80. Although the signal is somewhat long (at least three minutes), adhere to it. Approaching motorists don't expect bicyclists in their path when their light is green, and they take up virtually all of the road. By being impatient, you could cause a serious accident.

Continue riding north on Old Mine Road. Admire the beautiful river scenes on your left. You'll pass through Worthington State Forest and ride by a couple of picnic areas and campgrounds. You'll do a little climbing, but certainly nothing that will cause you much sweat.

It is twelve miles from the Visitor's Center to the restored village of Millbrook. Here, volunteers dress up the way Water Gap settlers did more than a hundred years ago. Lock up your bike and tour the village. Your first stop should be the Spangenberg Cabin, which acts as a small visitor's center for Millbrook Village. You can pick up a self-guided tour brochure that is helpful as you walk around Millbrook, and you can find out if there are any special activities going on during your visit. After Spangenberg Cabin, visit the Trauger House, the blacksmith shop, the general store, the gristmill, and the other restored buildings of Millbrook. This is a fine place to have a picnic and rest up for your return ride to the Delaware Water Gap Visitor's Center.

After your tour of Millbrook, begin the ride back to the Visitor's Center. There are no turns or specific directions other than to follow Old Mine Road to its end.

Great Swamp Swing

County:	Morris
Number of Miles:	16.6
Degree of Difficulty:	Moderate
Terrain:	Some hills
Surface:	Good
Things to See:	Village of New Vernon, Morris County Outdoor Education Center, Great Swamp Natural Wildlife Refuge, Wildlife Observation Center.

The Great Swamp Natural Wildlife Refuge is a delicate ecological preserve nestled in the southeast corner of Morris County. It's the end result of a huge glacial lake that once covered areas of Morris and Somerset counties more than 15,000 years ago.

Back in 1960, the Great Swamp almost became a fourth New York–New Jersey metropolitan area airport. But environmentalists and concerned citizens fought to save the Great Swamp and won. Today the Great Swamp is under the jurisdiction of the Department of the Interior. The 6,800-acre tract is the home of many wildlife and plant species as well as a resting place for migrating waterfowl.

The Great Swamp Swing tour is actually part of a larger tour put out in brochure form by the Bicycle Advocate's office of the New Jersey Department of Transportation. The tour of the Great Swamp consists of two loops. What follows is Loop #1.

The Great Swamp Swing begins in the village of New Vernon. Those arriving by car should look for parking near New Vernon's post office and small cluster of stores. Begin the tour by riding east (opposite the direction you came) on Village Road. You can expect some

Great Swamp Swing: Directions at a Glance

1. Village Road to Spring Valley Road.
2. Right onto Spring Valley/Green Village Road.
3. Right onto Hickory Place.
4. Right onto Southern Boulevard.
5. Right onto Fairmount Avenue.
6. Right onto Meyersville Road.
7. Right onto New Vernon Road, which turns into Long Hill Road.
8. Right onto Lee's Hill Road.
9. Right onto Village Road.

traffic on the road. Although it has no shoulder area, Village Road is wide enough so you won't have to compete with vehicles for your share of it. There is ample room for you to ride alongside traffic.

Continue on Village Road. You'll pass a connection with Pleasantville Road. Make a right at the stop sign onto Spring Valley Road. Spring Valley turns into Green Village Road. Follow Green Village Road to Hickory Place, a shortcut and alternative to dealing with the Shunpike Road/Southern Boulevard intersection a few hundred feet away at the stop sign.

Make a right onto Hickory Place and then another right onto a less hectic part of Southern Boulevard. Because Southern Boulevard winds across the boroughs of Madison and Chatham, you'll pass through a few residential areas. The Great Swamp Natural Wildlife Refuge is on your right, however.

Eventually you'll come to the Morris County Great Swamp Outdoor Center. A stop at the Center is recommended if you're interested in the ecology of the Great Swamp. At the Center you can view wildlife and natural history displays and special exhibits that deal with the formation of the swamp.

For bicyclists the only problem concerning the Outdoor Center is getting there. The driveway off Southern Boulevard that leads to the

Outdoor Center is rough and rocky. You'd be wise to walk your bike to the Center to safeguard against getting a flat tire.

After your visit to the Outdoor Center, return to Southern Boulevard. Turn right onto the boulevard and ride to the traffic light and intersection with Fairmount Avenue. Make a right and proceed down Fairmount to the intersection with Meyersville Road about a mile away.

Make a right onto Meyersville Road. Continue on it until you come to the intersection with New Vernon Road. Make a right on New Vernon and ride into the Great Swamp Natural Wildlife Refuge. A mile or so from the beginning of New Vernon Road, you'll come to the Wildlife Observation Center, where there are nature trails that lead farther into the heart of the Great Swamp. There is even a bike stand where you can lock your bike while hiking the trail.

Farther along New Vernon you'll come across more scenic views of the Great Swamp landscape. Depending on the season you might also spot migratory birds resting or feeding. New Vernon Road will turn into Long Hill Road once you leave the Great Swamp Refuge. Proceed on Long Hill to the intersection with Lee's Hill Road, sometimes referred to as Logansville Road. Make a right. A quarter mile down Lee's Hill Road will be the intersection with Village Road. Turn right here and proceed back into New Vernon where the tour began.

Tour of Tewksbury

County:	Hunterdon
Number of Miles:	17.7
Degree of Difficulty:	Moderate to difficult
Terrain:	Hills, some steep
Surface:	Good
Things to See:	Village of Oldwick, Oldwick General Store, Village of Mountainville, Mountainville General Store, Hunterdon County farm area

This tour is one of my favorites, especially in the fall when the trees of the Tewksbury section of Hunterdon County are a carnival of color. You'll ride on some of the prettiest country lanes in the state, stop at a general store for some fresh morning coffee and wonder why, in the past, you traveled all the way to Vermont and New Hampshire to admire their classic country landscapes when equally touching ones were right here in New Jersey.

The tour commences in Oldwick, a picturesque old village of antiques shops and restored country homes. First settled in the mid-eighteenth century, Oldwick was originally known as New Germantown.

Begin your ride on King's Street, the road between the Oldwick General Store and the Tewksbury Inn, a popular restaurant and drinking establishment. Proceed out of Oldwick on King's Street. Not far from the Oldwick General Store, you'll find yourself out in the country, where King's Street eventually turns into Potterstown Road. Don't be surprised if you spot a deer or two on your ride. The Oldwick area supports a healthy deer population.

Some two miles from Oldwick you'll come to a single-lane bridge. Proceed over it with caution. Just beyond the bridge is a stop sign at

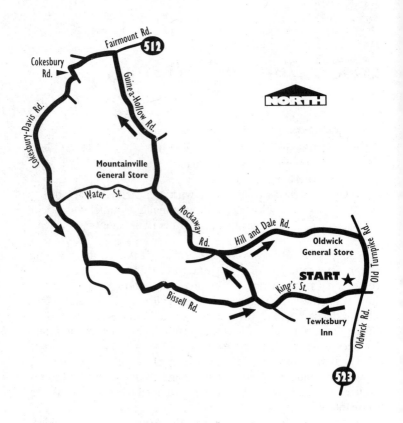

Fairmount Rd.

512

Cokesbury Rd.

Guinea-Hollow Rd.

Cokesbury-Davis Rd.

NORTH

Mountainville General Store

Water St.

Rockaway Rd.

Hill and Dale Rd.

Oldwick General Store

START ★

Old Turnpike Rd.

King's St.

Bissell Rd.

Tewksbury Inn

Oldwick Rd.

523

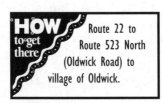

HOW to get there — Route 22 to Route 523 North (Oldwick Road) to village of Oldwick.

Tour of Tewksbury: Directions at a Glance

1. King's Street to Rockaway Road.
2. Right onto Rockaway Road.
3. Right at Water Street intersection.
4. Left onto Guinea-Hollow Road.
5. Left onto Fairmount Road.
6. Left onto Cokesbury Road.
7. Bear right at fork (onto Cokesbury–Davis Road).
8. Pass through two stop signs, bearing left at the first one and making a right at the second one to remain on Cokesbury-Davis Road.
9. Left onto Bissell Road.
10. Left onto Rockaway Road.
11. Right onto Hill and Dale Road.
12. Right onto Old Turnpike Road.

an intersection. Make a right here onto Rockaway Road. At the fork in the road a short distance away, bear to your right and continue on Rockaway Road. You will pass over a few more single-lane bridges.

At the "T" intersection and the corner of Rockaway Road and Water Street, you will come to the Mountainville General Store. If you're ready for something to drink or a bite to eat, this is a good place for it. If you're not, make a right at the "T" intersection. (It's a left if you crossed the intersection into the Mountainville General Store parking lot.)

Just on the outskirts of Mountainville is another single-lane bridge. Immediately after the bridge, make a left onto Guinea–Hollow Road. Proceed on Guinea–Hollow to the stop sign and "T" intersection. Make a left here onto Fairmount Road, also known as Route 512. Follow Fairmount to Cokesbury Road on the outskirts of the tiny village of Califon and make a left.

Be prepared for a steep climb up Cokesbury Road. At the top of the hill, you'll come to a fork in the road. Bear right onto Cokesbury–Davis Road. Follow this road to another fork; again bear to your right, which means you'll remain on Cokesbury–Davis Road. Much of this section of the tour is downhill, although there are a couple of slight inclines.

At the bottom of the hill, you'll come to a stop sign. Bear left. Shortly thereafter is another stop sign and intersection. This links Cokesbury Road and Water Street. Make a right and continue down Cokesbury Road to Bissell Road, where you'll make a left. On the way, you'll pass an old Methodist church and cemetery.

Proceed on Bissell Road. It's a winding country road with farms on both sides. Bear right at the Bissell Road–Still Hollow Road intersection, and continue on Bissell Road until its intersection with Rockaway Road a couple of miles later. Make a left onto Rockaway Road.

If this stretch of road looks familiar, it's because you rode on it earlier on your way to Mountainville. You won't be on it long, however. Make a right onto Hill and Dale Road, which is about a half mile away. Hill and Dale Road cuts through prime Hunterdon County farming area.

At the stop sign and intersection, make a right onto Old Turnpike Road, which in Oldwick becomes Oldwick Road. Old Turnpike Road is a fairly busy road for these parts since it eventually connects with Route 22. If you approached Oldwick and the start of this tour by car from Route 22, you took Route 523 to the Oldwick General Store.

Follow Old Turnpike Road into the village of Oldwick and to the Oldwick General Store. The tour ends here.

Round Valley Ramble

County:	Hunterdon
Number of Miles:	17.4
Degree of Difficulty:	Moderate
Terrain:	Hills
Surface:	Good
Things to See:	Village of Lebanon, Round Valley Recreation Area, Stanton General Store

Round Valley Recreation Area is made up of a huge, almost oval reservoir and more than 4,000 acres of park land in the middle of Hunterdon County. There are plenty of outdoor activities to be enjoyed here: wilderness camping, swimming, picnicking, boating, fishing, hiking, and scuba diving. Even though Round Valley doesn't have much in the way of bicycle paths or loops, the area and roads surrounding the reservoir more than make up for this deficiency.

The tour begins at the intersection of Main and Cherry streets in the village of Lebanon. Find a parking space along either of these streets. Proceed toward Round Valley by way of Cherry Street, which will take you out of Lebanon and into the countryside. Eventually, Cherry Street will turn into Route 629 (also known as Lebanon–Stanton Road). Once you reach Round Valley, you'll have a wonderful view of the reservoir and encompassing woodland.

At the stop sign make a left; you'll still be on Route 629. On weekends this part of Route 629 can get busy because it leads to the main entrance of Round Valley. Fortunately, there is adequate shoulder space to cycle on and stay out of any traffic you might encounter.

Proceed down Route 629 until you come to the entrance of the Round Valley Recreation Area. Make a left into the park and ride to the Visitor's Center. Unlike other state park visitor's centers, the one

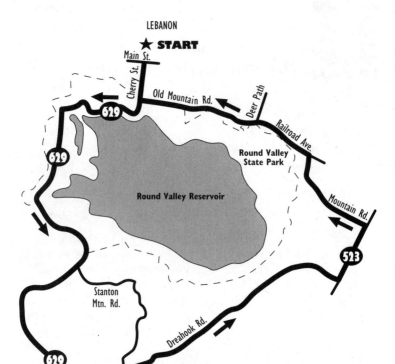

LEBANON

★ **START**

Main St.

Cherry St.

Old Mountain Rd.

Deer Path

Railroad Ave.

629

629

Round Valley Reservoir

Round Valley State Park

Mountain Rd.

523

Stanton Mtn. Rd.

Dreahook Rd.

629

Stanton General Store

NORTH

HOW to get there
Route 22 to Main Street in Lebanon.

Round Valley Ramble: Directions at a Glance

1. Cherry Street to Route 629.
2. Left at stop sign (still on Route 629).
3. Left into entrance of Round Valley Recreation Area.
4. Left onto Route 629.
5. Left onto Stanton Mountain Road.
6. Right onto Dreahook Road.
7. Left onto Route 523.
8. Left onto Mountain Road.
9. Left onto Railroad Avenue.
10. Left onto Old Mountain Road.
11. Right onto Cherry Street.

at Round Valley has little in the way of exhibits or displays. You can, however, pick up information on park activities and any special events going on as well as a map should you wish to do a bit of cycling in the park before continuing with the remainder of this tour. You can ride to the swimming and picnic areas and then turn around and come back to the Visitor's Center, where you'll follow the road to the entrance/exit of the park.

Make a left at the exit and continue on Route 629. You'll pass through scenic Hunterdon County countryside. You'll also pass through new residential areas dotted with high-priced homes where there once were working farms.

About six miles from the entrance to Round Valley Recreation Area, you'll come to the Stanton General Store. The General Store is one of only three public buildings in the tiny village of Stanton. The other two are the post office and church, and you'll pass both of them, too. But first stop at the General Store for a snack and something to drink.

Exit the General Store parking area onto Stanton Mountain Road. *Note:* You might recall that you passed an earlier entrance onto Stanton Mountain Road. That's because the road forms a half-loop as it

winds over Stanton Mountain (see map). A half mile or so later you'll make a right onto Dreahook Road. Continue on Dreahook, passing Round Valley Road and another residential area until you come to the "T" intersection. There is a stop sign here. Make a left onto Route 523 (Flemington–Whitehouse Road). A mile and a half from the Drea-hook/Route 523 intersection, make a left onto Mountain Road just beyond the Readington Township municipal complex. Ride to the second single-lane bridge. Immediately after the bridge, make a left onto Railroad Avenue. Railroad Avenue turns into Old Mountain Road after the Deer Path intersection. Make a left at this intersection and cross over the railroad tracks. On your immediate left will be the entrance to the Cushetunk Mountain Nature Preserve.

Proceed along Old Mountain Road. Round Valley is on your left. Approximately three miles from where you crossed the railroad tracks, you'll come to another intersection. Make a right here onto Cherry Street and ride back to Lebanon, where the tour concludes.

Flemington Flow

County:	Hunterdon
Number of Miles:	9
Degree of Difficulty:	Easy
Terrain:	Mostly flat
Surface:	Fair
Things to See:	Town of Flemington and its numerous historic buildings and shopping outlets, Hunterdon County countryside

Over the past twenty years Flemington has become more than the county seat of Hunterdon and western New Jersey's agriculture center. Once entrepreneurs realized the commercial potential of Flemington's Main Street with its many nineteenth-century buildings and classic small-town setting, Flemington quickly became a tourist and shopping attraction. Today, the town is bursting with outlet stores and boutiques that attract visitors from all over the New York–New Jersey metropolitan area.

There are other things to do in Flemington besides spend money, however. You can watch the glass cutters at work in the Flemington Cut Glass Company on Main Street. The County Courthouse, also on Main Street, was the site of the famous Lindbergh Trial in 1935, which attracted national attention. Bruno Hauptmann was convicted of the kidnapping and murder of the son of aviator Charles Lindbergh. Hauptmann was sentenced to death and later executed for his crimes.

You can also visit the Doric House (Maple Avenue and Main Street), home of the Hunterdon County Historical Society. Inside the house is a small museum. The Fleming Castle (Bonnell Street) once was a stagecoach depot and inn. The Daughters of the American Rev-

NORTH

Barley Sheaf Rd.

523

Flemington
Presbyterian
Church
START
★

31

523

E. Main St.

RARITAN RIVER

Rockafellow Mill Rd.

River Rd.

Pennsylvania Ave.

31

HOW
to get
there
Route 202 to Church Street
in Flemington. Right on Main
Street. Main Street to Presbyterian
Church on East Main Street.

Flemington Flow: Directions at a Glance

1. Left out of Presbyterian Church parking lot.
2. Cross over Route 31. Proceed on Route 523.
3. Left at stop sign. Continue on Route 523.
4. Right at "T" intersection (still Route 523).
5. Right onto Barley Sheaf Road.
6. Right onto Rockafellow Mill Road.
7. Right onto River Road at intersection immediately after Raritan River bridge.
8. River Road to Pennsylvania Avenue.
9. Pennsylvania Avenue to Route 31. Cross over Route 31.
10. Pennsylvania Avenue to East Main Street.
11. Right on East Main Street.
12. Left back into Presbyterian Church parking lot.

---

olution conduct tours of Fleming Castle, but only by appointment. (Call 908–782–4655.)

It is possible to bicycle through the side streets of Flemington and admire the town's many historic buildings, but this tour begins on the edge of Main Street's shopping area and continues through the countryside on the outskirts of town.

The tour begins in the parking lot of the Flemington Presbyterian Church on East Main Street. Ride out the driveway and proceed down East Main Street, away from the center of Flemington. A half mile later you'll come to the Route 31 intersection and traffic light. Cross over Route 31. You will now be on Route 523. Follow Route 523 (Flemington–Junction Road). Admittedly, this part of the tour isn't very scenic. The area is a combination of old and new Flemington and reveals the industry that has settled here.

At the stop sign, make a left. You are still on Route 523. At the "T" intersection and stop sign, make a right. You're still on Route 523. (If you turned left, you would be on Route 612.) Pass the Lipton Tea Company plant on your right and cross over the Raritan River. Follow Route 523 to Barley Sheaf Road, where you'll make a right.

The scenery improves considerably in this section of the tour. Years ago this was all farmland. Today development has occurred here, but not enough to destroy the largely agricultural setting for which Hunterdon County is known.

Make a right onto Rockafellow Mill Road. You'll cross over two sets of railroad tracks and recross the Raritan River. As you cross the bridge, look to your right at the small waterfall. Make a right at the intersection immediately after the bridge onto River Road, and you'll be riding parallel to the Raritan River.

Up ahead not quite a mile, you'll come to Pennsylvania Avenue. Proceed on Pennsylvania Avenue. Your next intersection will be at Route 31. Cross over Route 31. You're still on Pennsylvania Avenue. Take Pennsylvania Avenue to East Main Street where the tour began. East Main Street is the second stop sign on Pennsylvania Avenue. Make a right onto East Main Street and a left back into the Presbyterian Church parking lot. This ends the tour.

Note: This tour is courtesy of the Hunterdon County Park System. It is number 9 of the series of tours the Park System publishes for bicyclists who wish to explore in depth the back roads of Hunterdon, arguably the state's best county for bicycling.

Stockton Covered Bridge Tour

County:	Hunterdon
Number of Miles:	19.4
Degree of Difficulty:	Moderate
Terrain:	Hills, some steep
Surface:	Good
Things to See:	Stockton, Hunterdon County farmland, Covered Bridge, Rosemont General Store, Delaware & Raritan Canal, Delaware River

Stockton is a little hamlet nestled on the banks of the Delaware River, just a couple of miles north of Lambertville's shopping district. Many of the homes found in Stockton date back 150 years or more, and there is a cheery warmth to the town that reminds one of New England, especially Vermont.

Those who already know Stockton probably do so because of the Stockton Inn (formerly Colligan's Stockton Inn), a popular bed-and-breakfast–style hotel. Established in the early eighteenth century, the inn was made somewhat famous in this century when Richard Rodgers, of the great American songwriting team of Rodgers and Hart, wrote his song "There's a Small Hotel with a Wishing Well" while visiting the Stockton Inn. The wishing well Rodgers wrote about is still on the premises, and virtually everyone who eats or stays at the inn throws a penny or two in it for good luck.

This tour begins in Stockton, just across from the Stockton Inn. The Inn is located on Route 29. Park your car in front of the small cluster of shops on Bridge Street, Stockton's one and only business area, which faces the Stockton Inn. Notice the bridge two hundred yards away to the west. It connects Stockton with Pennsylvania's Bucks County. Wine lovers should also browse through Phillips's, the

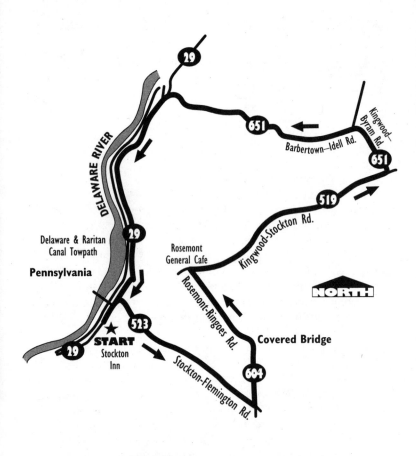

Stockton–Covered Bridge Tour: Directions at a Glance

1. Left onto Route 29.
2. Bear right at fork onto Route 523 (Stockton–Flemington Road).
3. Left onto Rosemont-Ringoes Road (Route 604).
4. Right onto Kingwood–Stockton Road (Route 519).
5. Left onto Route 651 South (Kingwood–Byram Road).
6. Left onto Route 29.
7. Bear right at intersection just outside Stockton.
8. Right onto Bridge Street (across from the Stockton Inn).

liquor store on Bridge Street. The selection of wines there is truly outstanding, especially for such a small town as Stockton.

Make a left onto Route 29 North to start this tour and proceed to the fork in the road not more than a couple hundred yards away. Bear right at the fork onto Route 523. The sign at this intersection will indicate that Route 523 is the way to Flemington and Sergeantsville. You'll now pedal up your first hill of this tour, and it's a good one. Near the top you'll see a sign for the Woolverton Inn. This is the second of Stockton's popular bed & breakfast inns. Unlike the Stockton Inn, though, the Woolverton's setting is purely rural.

Proceed on Route 523, which is also called the Stockton–Flemington Road, until the intersection of Route 604. On the way you'll pass working farms, cornfields, picturesque rolling hills, and for many, a view of New Jersey that they thought never existed. If you ever doubted why New Jersey is nicknamed the Garden State, this tour should set aside those doubts.

Make a left onto Route 604, which is also called the Rosemont–Ringoes Road, in the tiny village of Sergeantsville. Sergeantsville was first settled around 1700. It was named for a local Revolutionary War patriot and soldier, Charles Sergeant.

Just down the road on Route 604 you'll come to New Jersey's only

remaining covered bridge, the Green–Sergeant Bridge. At one time there were seventy-five covered bridges in the state. This one, built in the early eighteenth century, is now a New Jersey landmark. You'll find a photograph of it in just about every brochure published by New Jersey's Division of Travel and Tourism that relates to Hunterdon County and Jersey's scenic country roads.

Pedal over the covered bridge and continue on the Rosemont–Ringoes Road (Route 604) until the "T" intersection a couple of miles away. Rosemont–Ringoes Road runs into the Kingwood–Stockton Road, also known as Route 519. But before you make a right onto Kingwood–Stockton Road, pay a visit to the Rosemont General Cafe, where a traditional country breakfast awaits you, or at the very least, a cup of freshly brewed coffee. The Rosemont General Cafe can get busy on weekend mornings, especially Sundays. Thus, it is best to arrive early.

Make a right and proceed north on the Kingwood–Stockton Road (Route 519), once again passing picture-perfect country scenes, stone houses more than two hundred years old, small farms, and in the fall, the beautiful foliage. Make a left onto Route 651 South (Kingwood–Byram Road), a few miles beyond the Rosemont General Cafe. At the "T" intersection bear left and continue on Route 651 South. (At this point Route 651 is called Barbertown–Idell Road. Later, it will change back to Kingwood–Byram Road.) Be prepared for more hills. But there is a reward for all your hard pedaling: The last part of Route 651, which leads back to Route 29 and the Delaware River, is almost all downhill.

Make a left onto Route 29. Even though Route 29 is a heavily used highway south of Lambertville, since it connects that town with Trenton, this stretch of Route 29 contains much less traffic. And unlike the Lambertville–Trenton section, this section of Route 29 has a smooth, spacious shoulder, ideal for bicycle riding.

You will be able to keep a good, strong pace on Route 29 as you ride back to Stockton. Those wishing for a slower route back to Stockton might opt for riding on the Delaware & Raritan Canal Towpath, which is to your right as you head south on Route 29. You'll see a sign indicating the Delaware & Raritan Canal State Park, Bull's Island Recreation Area soon after the intersection of Routes 651 and 29. At the sign and entrance to the park, make a right, pick up the towpath (which, by the way, is the same towpath described in the Lambertville Loop), and ride back to Stockton.

Those of you on Route 29 will pass the Prallsville Mills, a renovated nineteenth-century industrial center worth investigating. After visiting the Prallsville Mills, continue on Route 29 to the intersection outside Stockton. Make a right here and follow signs to Lambertville. An eight of a mile later, this time at the Stockton Inn, make a right onto Bridge Street, thus concluding your tour.

Lambertville Loop

County:	Mercer
Number of Miles:	23
Degree of Difficulty:	Moderate to difficult
Terrain:	Hills
Surface:	Mostly good, but some rough spots
Things to See:	Lambertville, Delaware River, Delaware & Raritan Canal, Howell Farm, scenic country-side of Mercer County, Marshall House, Lambertville House

Lambertville, like its sister town New Hope, is filled with antiques shops and art galleries, cafes and boutiques, restored rowhouses and riverfront recreation. New Hope, located just across the Delaware River in Pennsylvania, is the more popular town, and its distinction as an artists' colony is certainly widespread in the mid-Atlantic region. But, if Lambertville doesn't quite carry the reputation of its counterpart, perhaps that is what makes it more special.

On weekends, Lambertville is less crowded than New Hope and offers less in the way of commercial hype. You can stroll Lambertville's streets without constantly bumping into people. You don't have to wait too long to be seated in its most noted cafes and restaurants during lunch and dinner.

Lambertville is one of the oldest towns in Hunterdon County. Early on it turned to manufacturing as a means of income for its residents. Canning, shoe, and rubber factories dominated the landscape, and their owners hired local men to work them. In 1859 the Lambertville Iron Works opened and continued to operate for almost fifty years.

Today such industries are not part of Lambertville's makeup. But some of the factory buildings have been renovated and turned into

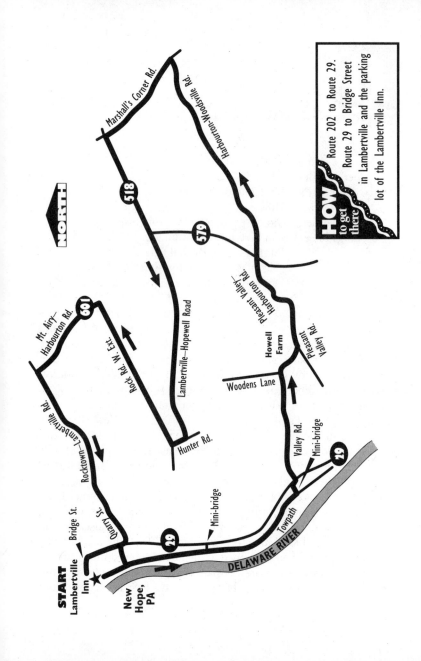

Lambertville Loop: Directions at a Glance

1. Left side of Lambertville Inn—gravel road.
2. Gravel road to Delaware & Raritan Canal Towpath.
3. Left at second bridge over Delaware & Raritan Canal Towpath.
4. Walk up path to Route 29. Cross over Route 29 to Valley Road.
5. Valley Road to Woodens Lane and Howell Living History Farm.
6. Left onto Woodens Lane and enter Howell Living History Farm.
7. Return back to Woodens Lane after visit to Howell Living History Farm.
8. Left onto Valley Road.
9. Left onto Pleasant Valley Road.
10. Left onto Pleasant Valley–Harbourton Road.
11. Left onto Marshall's Corner Road.
12. Left onto Lambertville–Hopewell Road (Route 518).
13. Right onto Rock Road W. Ext.
14. Left onto Mt. Airy–Harbourton Road (Route 601).
15. Left onto Rocktown–Lambertville Road (Quarry Street).
16. Right at conclusion of Rocktown–Lambertville Road (Quarry Street).
17. Left at traffic light onto Bridge Street.
18. Bridge Street to Lambertville Inn parking lot.

clusters of clothing and kitchenware outlet shops, while many of the rowhouses where factory workers lived have been given wonderful facelifts.

It would be a good idea to plan on a full day to complete this tour, for two reasons. First, it's a rather long one, with many hills. Second, after you've ridden it, you'll surely want to spend some time in Lambertville browsing through its shops and galleries.

Complete the Lambertville Loop in the morning. You'll ride on the Delaware & Raritan Canal Towpath and back into the nearby Mercer County countryside. (Lambertville is located in Hunterdon County, it's true. But it sits on Hunterdon's southern boundary. For a country lane tour of Hunterdon County, see the Stockton–Covered Bridge Tour.)

After you've completed the tour, have lunch in any of Lambertville's fine eateries. The Inn at the Lambertville Station is highly recommended. Then, spend the rest of the afternoon in Lambertville, and if time permits, New Hope.

For those wishing to make a weekend of it all, there are two good bed & breakfasts in Lambertville—the Bridge Street House and the York Street House—plus a fine hotel, the Lambertville Inn, which possesses all the amenities of a first-class hotel, but with the cozy charm of a small inn.

In fact, this tour begins in the parking lot of the Lambertville Inn, located on the banks of the Delaware River off Bridge Street. Off to the side of the inn, the side opposite the river, is a gravel road that leads to the Delaware & Raritan Canal Towpath. The Towpath, as you'll recall if you've ridden the Stockton Covered Bridge Tour or the Washington Crossing State Park tour, is a unique bicycle path.

The gravel road that leads to the Towpath often contains loose chunks of gravel and potholes. With the exception of Woodens Lane farther on in the tour, this gravel road is the worst road condition you'll encounter. If you own an all-terrain or mountain bike, you might consider using it for this tour. But a ten-speed with good tires will certainly do, too. You'll probably meet a few cyclists riding both kinds of bikes on the Towpath.

At the end of the gravel road, you'll come to a gate. It is there to prevent vehicles from riding on the Towpath. Walk your bike around the gate and resume riding. You will pass one mini-bridge over the Delaware & Raritan Canal on your left. The Delaware River is on your right. About a mile from the gate, you will find another bridge. Cross over this bridge and walk your bike up the short but steep path. You'll find yourself on the shoulder of Route 29.

Cross over Route 29, but do so with caution because it is a busy road, especially in this section. You will now be at the base of Valley Road. Here you'll see an old stone barn and signs for Howell Farm and the Belle Mountain Ski Area.

Valley Road is a long, winding hill that will take you to Howell

Farm, your first stop. Along the way you'll pass the Belle Mountain Ski Area on your right. At the intersection of Valley Road and Woodens Lane, approximately one and a half miles from the bottom of Valley Road, make a left, following signs to the entrance of Howell Farm.

Howell Farm is a "living history" farm. (See also Longstreet Farm in the Holmdel Hustle tour.) A "living history" farm means that there are farm animals and fields of crops and that many of the chores are performed in a traditional, nineteenth-century manner. Run by the Mercer County Parks Commission, Howell Farm is also the site of occasional farm-related events such as a pumpkin-picking festival in October and hayrides.

Visit the farmhouse adjacent to the main barn and barnyard. These areas are typical of daily existence on a farm a century ago, and they reveal how a local farm family worked and lived.

Return to Woodens Lane, make a left, and go back to Valley Road. Make another left at Valley Road and continue down it to the "T" intersection with Pleasant Valley Road. Make yet another left and continue on Pleasant Valley Road.

The many rolling hills that you'll ride up and down throughout the next part of this tour possess some of the prettiest rural scenery in New Jersey. You'll pass many farms and fields, and don't be surprised if you spot a deer or two in the brush.

Your next turn, a left, will be onto Pleasant Valley–Harbourton Road, a couple of miles from the Valley Road/Pleasant Valley Road intersection. This is not a major intersection, so keep a sharp eye out for it. There is, however, a visible street sign.

Continue on Pleasant Valley–Harbourton Road. Cross over Route 579, the next intersection. Pleasant Valley–Harbourton Road now becomes Harbourton–Woodsville Road. You'll eventually come to another intersection where Harbourton–Woodsville Road intersects with Marshall's Corner Road. At last look, there was no marker or sign indicating Marshall's Corner Road. Across from where Harbourton–Woodsville Road intersects with Marshall's Corner Road is a small housing development; the name of the road leading into it is Fox Run Road. Use the Fox Run Road sign as your guide for Marshall's Corner Road. Make a left onto Marshall's Corner Road and proceed to the

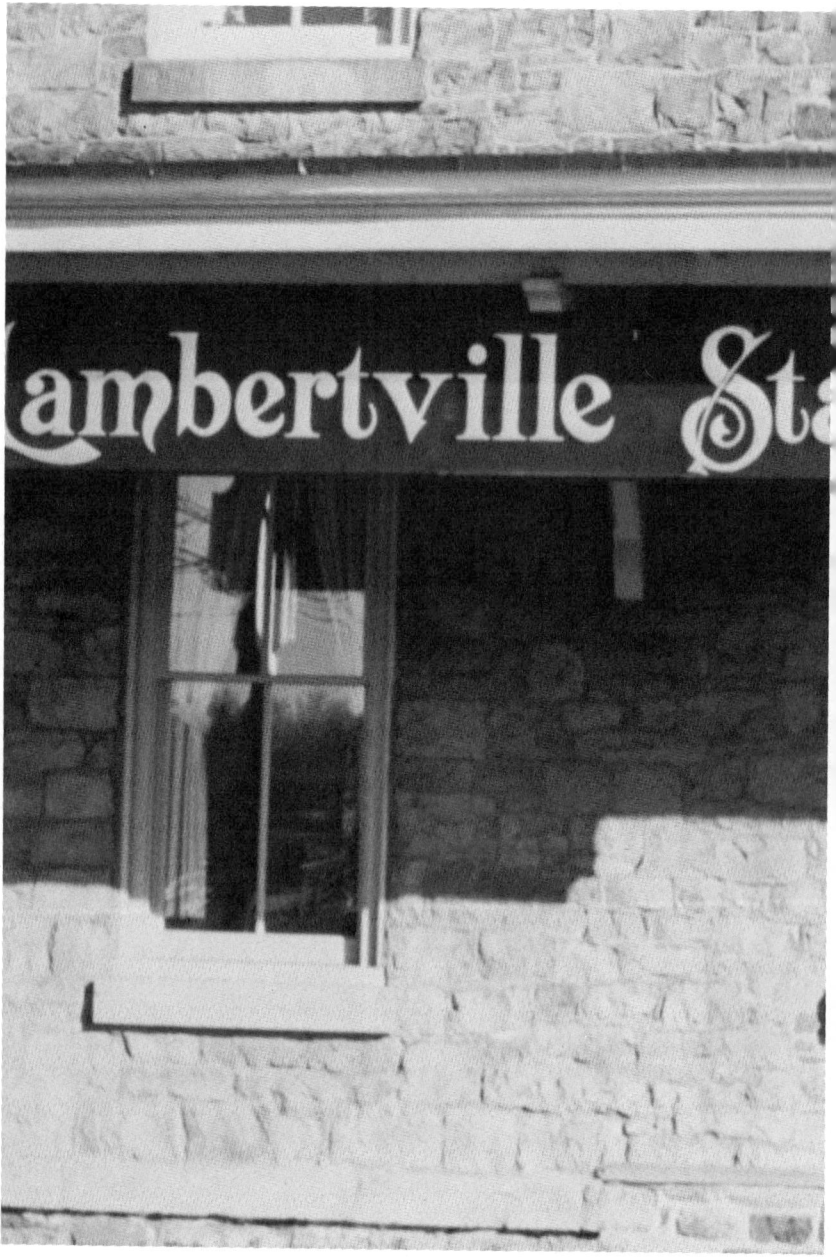
Lambertville Sta

blinking traffic light and Route 518, where you'll make a left turn. Route 518 is also known as the Lambertville–Hopewell Road; eventually it becomes Brunswick Pike. There should be a sign for Lambertville; it points in the direction you are headed.

Proceed on Route 518. It is a semi-busy road, so be careful. A few miles up on Route 518, you'll come to the Route 518 and Hunter Road–Rock Road intersection. (The left side of the intersection is Hunter Road; the right side is Rock Road W. Ext.) You'll be able to identify the intersection because on your left is a bicycle shop called Wheel Fine Cycling. Make a right onto Rock Road. Rock Road will take you through a forested area of Hunterdon County. (Yes, you're back in Hunterdon County.) At the stop sign a few miles down the road, make a left. You'll now be on Mt. Airy–Harbourton Road, also known as Route 601.

Continue on Mt. Airy–Harbourton Road until the intersection with Rocktown–Lambertville Road, which eventually becomes Quarry Street. Make, what else, but a left. This road will take you straight into Lambertville, and it's all downhill.

At the stop sign on the edge of Lambertville, and the end of the Rocktown–Lambertville Road (Quarry Street), make a right. This is a busy intersection; be wary of traffic. At the traffic light two hundred yards or so up ahead, make a left onto Bridge Street.

If there is too much traffic and not enough room to ride with safety, walk your bike through downtown Lambertville back to the Lambertville Station, a few short blocks away. On your right you'll pass the James Wilson Marshall House, the childhood home of the man who, with his partner Augustus Sutter, discovered gold in California in 1848. This discovery, of course, led to the famous California Gold Rush.

A block later you'll pass the Lambertville House, also on your right. Built in 1812, it hosted such great men in American history as President Andrew Johnson and General U. S. Grant.

Proceed on Bridge Street to the Lambertville Station and the Inn at the Lambertville Station, where you'll make a left into the parking lot and conclude the tour.

Washington Crossing State Park

County:	Mercer
Number of Miles:	8.5
Degree of Difficulty:	Easy
Terrain:	Mostly flat
Surface:	Mostly good
Things to See:	Delaware River, Delaware & Raritan Canal, Nelson House, Titusville, Washington Crossing State Park, Visitor's Center, Ferry House, George Washington Memorial Arboretum

This tour is steeped in American history. At what is today Washington Crossing State Park, General George Washington and his Continental troops made their famous river-crossing on Christmas night, 1776. Their attack on the Hessian mercenaries in Trenton was a turning point in America's battle for independence, according to most historians. Your tour is almost wholly within Washington Crossing State Park.

Located about midway between Lambertville and Trenton, Washington Crossing State Park is one of the state's prettiest parks. Beautifully maintained with much to see and do, the park is on the banks of the Delaware River and the land just beyond it and truly beckons bicyclists. Next to the park is the small, picturesque village of Titusville and a stretch of the Delaware & Raritan Canal and Towpath, all of which are included in this tour.

Since there is so much for the touring cyclist to experience here, if possible plan to make a full day out of your bicycle ride and visit to the park. You'll certainly want to spend time at the Visitor's Center and other places of interest along the tour, and there are plenty of places to picnic.

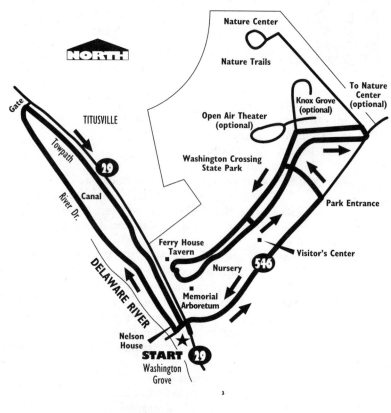

NORTH

Nature Center

Nature Trails

TITUSVILLE

Towpath

29

Canal

River Dr.

To Nature
Center
(optional)

Knox Grove
(optional)

Open Air Theater
(optional)

Gate

Washington Crossing
State Park

Park Entrance

DELAWARE RIVER

Ferry House
Tavern

Nursery

546

Visitor's Center

Nelson
House

Memorial
Arboretum

START 29

Washington
Grove

3

HOW to get there
Route 29 to the
Route 546 intersection and
the Washington Grove entrance
to Washington Crossing State Park.

Washington Crossing State Park: Directions at a Glance

1. Washington Grove parking lot onto River Drive into Titusville.
2. River Drive to Delaware & Raritan Canal Towpath; return to Washington Grove via Towpath.
3. Cross over Route 29. Route 546 to entrance; enter Washington Crossing State Park.
4. Left at second stop sign in park; proceed toward Visitor's Center. Enter Visitor's Center parking lot.
5. Right out of Visitor's Center parking lot and proceed to stop sign intersection. Follow signs for Nature Center, Knox Grove, and Open Air Theater. Follow road around this section of the park and back to the main entrance/exit road.
6. Cross main entrance/exit road, and once again, follow signs to Visitor's Center.
7. Do not turn into Visitor's Center parking lot. Instead continue to Ferry House Tavern and George Washington Memorial Arboretum. (Follow signs.)
8. Once again, return to main entrance/exit road. Make a right at the stop sign and proceed out of the park.
9. Right onto Route 546.
10. Cross over Route 29 and make a right into Washington Grove parking lot.

If you come during the summer, you might want to stay for a play or concert at the Washington Crossing Open Air Theater located in the park. For information on theatrical and musical performances, call (609) 737–9721. Also, you might want to pedal over to Washington Crossing's sister park in Pennsylvania, where further history pertaining to Washington and his army and their daring winter crossing of the Delaware River awaits you.

The tour commences just outside the main section of Washington

Crossing State Park, off Route 29 in what's known as Washington Grove. Directly opposite the road that leads to the formal entrance of the park (Route 546) is a bridge that spans the Delaware River and leads into Pennsylvania. If you're coming from Trenton, make a left at the traffic light, which is the Route 29–Route 546 intersection. Just before the bridge, which is not more than 200 feet away, is the entrance to Washington Grove. Make a right here. You will now be in the parking lot adjacent to the Nelson House. (If you're coming from Lambertville and points north, make a right at the Route 29–Route 546 traffic light and then the quick right into Washington Grove as stated above. Do not go over the bridge.)

Before embarking on your ride, pay a brief visit to the Nelson House. The Nelson House was the landing point for the ferry to Pennsylvania before a covered bridge was built and made ferry service at this point on the river obsolete. The building served as the ferryman's residence as well as a tavern for those waiting for the ferry. Directly across from the Nelson House is the actual point where Washington and his troops landed on Christmas night, 1776. The plaque located by this site explains the details pertaining to the crossing.

Approximately 2,400 Continental soldiers crossed the river that night. With them, they brought supplies and eight cannon. After the battle, in which 900 Hessians were captured and another 100 killed or wounded, Washington and his men, along with their Hessian captives, recrossed the Delaware at this point.

Once you've digested this bit of historical information, ride to the end of the parking lot, opposite its entrance. There you will find a scenic road, River Drive, which takes you along the Delaware and through the town of Titusville.

Titusville resembles a scene right out of a Norman Rockwell painting. Well-kept colonial homes hug the banks of the Delaware, and a sense of history and Americana surrounds the small community. It is only one and one-half miles from the start of the tour to the north end of Titusville. At this point, you'll bear right and return to the Nelson House and the Washington Grove parking lot. But this time you'll ride by way of the Delaware & Raritan Canal Towpath. The Towpath runs parallel to River Drive, but instead of being on the

Delaware River, it is on the Delaware & Raritan Canal, located behind the river section of Titusville that you just rode through.

Do not go over the small canal bridge, located to the right of the conclusion of River Drive. If you do, you'll go onto Route 29, a busy highway too dangerous for cyclists, at least this section of it. Just before the canal bridge, you'll see the Towpath. It will, most likely, have a wooden gate across it to prevent cars from entering. Simply walk your bicycle around it and ride the Towpath back to Washington Grove.

Upon completion of the Towpath section of the tour, make a left and go up to the traffic light located at the Route 29–Route 546 intersection. Cross over Route 29 and begin your pedal up the Route 546 hill to the formal entrance of Washington Crossing State Park, about three-quarters of a mile away. Make a left into the entrance of the park. Pass the stop sign intersection a short distance away.

A couple hundred feet farther is another intersection. Make a left at the stop sign here and follow signs to the Visitor's Center. Make another left into the Visitor's Center parking lot. Notice that the lot is located about 150 yards from the Visitor's Center building. Leave your locked bike in the parking lot and walk to the Visitor's Center, or walk with your bike along the path that leads to the building and lock it there.

In the Visitor's Center you'll be able to browse through two museum galleries that contain some 900 Revolutionary War artifacts. The North Gallery comprises items that deal with Washington's crossing of the Delaware and the Battle of Trenton. The theme of the South Gallery is New Jersey's role in the Revolution. The impressive collection of artifacts is chronological in arrangement. There are twelve sub-themes, which begin with "Prelude to Revolution: 1758–73" and end with "Results of the Revolution: 1781–83."

There is also an electric map that details the crossing and ensuring battle and a wonderful twenty-minute film that depicts in dramatic fashion still more crossing and battle information.

After you've spent some time in the Visitor's Center, where you can also pick up free park maps and brochures, return to the parking lot area. Ride out of the parking lot, following the exit signs. Cross the intersection at the stop sign and continue to the Nature Center, Knox Grove, and Open Air Theater. At the bend in the road, you'll see the detour for the Nature Center. Visit it if you wish, but be advised that the road leading to it is not a good one.

Continue around the bend. Soon you'll come to the entrance to Knox Grove and the Open Air Theater. Once again, visit these if you wish. Knox Grove is a good place for a picnic in Washington Crossing State Park. It is situated on a loop road that will return you to where you are now.

Just beyond this point, on your right, you'll come to the Spring House. It's a small stone structure that once stood over a cold spring. Eighteenth-century farmers kept milk and other perishables in structures of this kind.

Proceed to the stop sign and the intersection of the park's main road. Cross the intersection; once again follow signs to the Visitor's Center. You have already cycled this stretch of the park. But rather than turning into the Visitor's Center parking lot as before, ride down the road to the Ferry House Tavern and Memorial Arboretum.

At the bottom of this road, you'll see the Ferry House Tavern. This is your next stop. It was here that General Washington set up his command post and discussed battle strategy with his officers on Christmas night. Across from the Ferry House is a stone barn from the original farm that was here during the Revolutionary War. Also near the Ferry House Tavern is the George Washington Memorial Arboretum; it contains trees and shrubs native to New Jersey.

Continue on this road, which passes the nursery north of the Arboretum. Pass, too, the Visitor's Center. Return to the next stop sign intersection. Make a right and ride to the park's exit. Make another right onto Route 546 and ride down the hill with caution. Cross the Route 29–Route 546 intersection at the light and return to the Nelson House and Washington Grove parking area, where the tour began.

Cheesequake State Park

County:	Middlesex
Number of Miles:	9.5
Degree of Difficulty:	Easy
Terrain:	Flat, except for Booth Field Road
Surface:	Mostly good, except for Booth Field Road
Things to See:	Cheesequake State Park natural areas, wildlife sanctuary, Hooks Lake

There are few scenic cycling areas in Middlesex County. Middlesex is a crossroads county; many of the state's major highways, including the New Jersey Turnpike, Garden State Parkway, and Routes 287, 1, 9, and 18, intersect each other here. And recent development, both residential and commercial, has been widespread.

There is, however, a suitable cycling area in Cheesequake State Park, located in northeastern Middlesex County. The name "Cheesequake" can be traced back to the area's original inhabitants, the Leni-Lenape Indians. Although Cheesequake State Park is small in comparison to other state parks and possesses no historic sites or other major attractions, it is, nonetheless, a good place to cycle, especially during the fall when the trees of Cheesequake explode with color.

Cheesequake is also easily accessible for bicyclists who live in Middlesex and upper Monmouth counties. It is an island in the middle of what is one of New Jersey's fastest-growing suburban areas and, thus, can be enjoyed by a large number of bicycle tourists.

Actually, the Cheesequake State Park tour begins outside the park. If you arrive by car, park it in the commuter parking lot adjacent to the exit 120 ramp off the Garden State Parkway South. You can also arrive at the lot via the Laurence Harbor Parkway, which crosses underneath the Garden State Parkway.

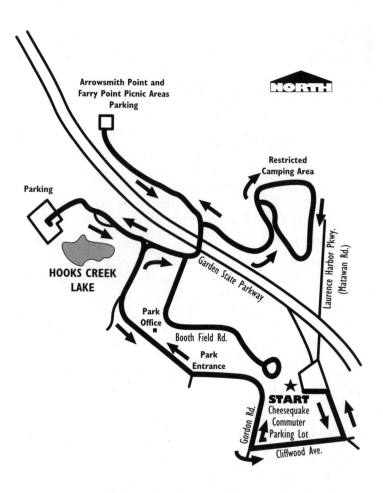

Arrowsmith Point and
Farry Point Picnic Areas
Parking

NORTH

Restricted
Camping Area

Parking

Laurence Harbor Pkwy.
(Matawan Rd.)

**HOOKS CREEK
LAKE**

Garden State Parkway

Park
Office

Booth Field Rd.

Park
Entrance

Gordon Rd.

★ **START**
Cheesequake
Commuter
Parking Lot

Cliffwood Ave.

HOW to get there — Garden State Parkway
South, exit 120 to
Cheesequake Commuter
Parking Lot.

Cheesequake: Directions at a Glance

1. Exit commuter parking lot adjacent to exit 120 south ramp off Garden State Parkway. Bear right onto Laurence Harbor Parkway (Matawan Road).
2. Right at traffic light onto Cliffwood Avenue.
3. Right onto Gordon Road.
4. Bear right at first bend in road after passing park headquarters.
5. Right at stop sign.
6. Bear left at next intersection. Head toward Arrowsmith Point and Farry Point.
7. U-turn in Farry Point parking lot.
8. Proceed into Restricted Camping Area. Ride loop road.
9. Bear left at intersection just beyond Restricted Camping Area gates.
10. Left at stop sign.
11. Left onto Booth Field Road.
12. U-turn in Booth Field parking area.
13. Left onto main road in park.
14. Bear left at small island just beyond the entrance/exit road of park.
15. Proceed to Hooks Lake.
16. U-turn in Hooks Lake parking area.
17. Right at entrance/exit road intersection and proceed out of park onto Gordon Road.
18. Left onto Cliffwood Avenue.
19. Left onto Laurence Harbor Parkway (Matawan Road).

Exit the parking lot and bear right onto Laurence Harbor Parkway, also known as Matawan Road. The road sign will say "Matawan and Old Bridge Township, Route 34." A quarter mile down the road, make a right at the traffic light onto Cliffwood Avenue. Proceed a half mile or so to the traffic light. Make a right here onto Gordon Road. This road will lead to the entrance of the park.

Before proceeding into the park, stop at the Ranger Headquarters, which is located to the right of the park entrance booth. Pick up a Cheesequake park brochure and map. Exit the headquarters' parking lot and ride into Cheesequake.

Bear right at the first bend in the road and proceed to the V-shaped island in the middle of the road. There will also be a stop sign there. Make a right and continue farther into the park. You'll ride under both the southern and northern lanes of the Garden State Parkway.

At the next intersection, bear left and head toward Arrowsmith Point and Farry Point, two picnic areas in the northeast corner of Cheesequake. Pass through the Farry Point gates and pedal to the Farry Point picnic area, a half mile or so up the road.

Unlike most other parks that possess "loop" or circular roads and thus eliminate backtracking, Cheesequake has a series of roads that lead to a particular destination and dead end. Such is the case here. When you arrive at Farry Point, make a U-turn in the picnic area parking lot and return on the same road to the intersection. Instead of bearing right, however, and following the signs to New Landing and Hooks Lake, continue straight and ride into the Restricted Camping Area. This is the only loop-like ride in Cheesequake. It will take you on a quick tour of the campsites. Stay on the paved road and loop the campground. Once you're into the campground area, simply follow the exit signs and return to the same Restricted Camping Area gates you entered through.

Just beyond the gates is the intersection mentioned earlier. If you proceed straight, you'll head back to Farry Point. So, bear left and then make a left at the stop sign. Proceed under the Garden State Parkway again. Shortly thereafter is a road on your left that leads to the Booth Field Camping Area.

This road has had pothole problems in the past; there is no guarantee that your ride up this road will be a smooth and easy one. And you'll have to do a bit of climbing because Booth Field sits atop a hill.

Those who prefer not to strain a bit or who decide against battling the possible potholes should bypass this road and continue toward Hooks Lake, your next destination. For those with a bit of adventure in their blood, make a left onto the Booth Field Road, pedal to the top, admire the foliage along the way as well as the tiny chipmunks that will scurry across the road in front of you, and then turn around and pedal on down.

Make a left back onto the main road and continue to Hooks Lake. You'll pass the road that leads back to the entrance/exit of the park. Bear left at the small island just beyond the entrance/exit road and follow signs to the lake.

There is swimming at Hooks Lake during the summer. There is also a large picnic area. If you plan to spend the day at Cheesequake, this is a good place for a respite. There are also several interesting hiking trails in the vicinity. Cheesequake is located in the "transition zone" of northern and southern New Jersey's vegetation regions. You'll find marsh areas, swamps, and a sample of Pine Barrens forest here, as well as a section of hardwood forest.

As might be expected, on weekends this part of Cheesequake can get crowded, so plan accordingly. Turn around in the parking lot and backtrack to the entrance/exit road intersection. Make a right and proceed out of Cheesequake and onto Gordon Road. At the traffic light, make a left onto Cliffwood Avenue. At the next traffic light, make another left onto Laurence Harbor Parkway (Matawan Road) and pedal back to the commuter parking lot where the tour began.

Highlands Hilltopper

County:	Monmouth
Number of Miles:	6.2
Degree of Difficulty:	Moderate to difficult
Terrain:	Mostly hills, some steep
Surface:	Good
Things to See:	Atlantic Highlands, Scenic Drive, Mt. Mitchill, views of Sandy Hook and Sandy Hook Bay

Don't let the number of miles fool you. This is a short, but fairly strenuous tour. There are a number of tough hills on Ocean Boulevard. But for some bicyclists, the sweeping vistas at Mt. Mitchill and other points atop the Highlands make the effort worthwhile. The Highlands and the roads that comprise this tour are close to Sandy Hook and the Navesink River (see Sandy Hook and Navesink River Ramble tours). Cyclists interested in making a weekend out of touring might want to try all three tours or combine at least two of them into a good day's ride.

This tour concentrates on the scenic views of Sandy Hook and Sandy Hook Bay. It begins in the town of Atlantic Highlands, a popular boating and fishing outlet for charters, party boats, and private pleasure craft. The tour commences in the Municipal Harbor parking area at the very end of First Avenue. Park your car here.

Ride out of the parking area by way of Simon Lake Drive, which is the road closest to the docks. You'll pass the Shore Casino, a noted Atlantic Highlands restaurant. Proceed on Simon Lake Drive and ride around the bend, where the view on a clear day is spectacular. Look for the Verrazano Bridge, Brooklyn, and Manhattan. At the conclusion of the bend, Simon Lake Drive merges into First Avenue.

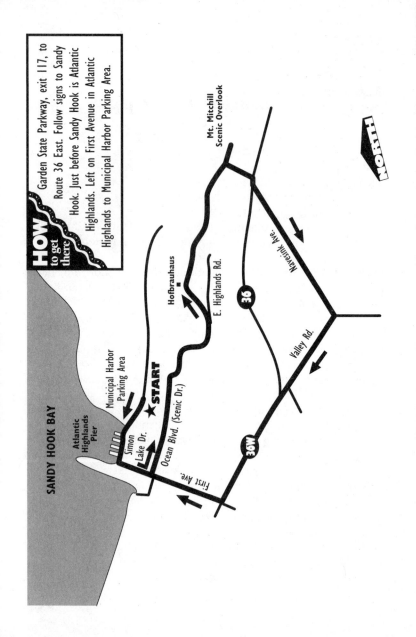

HOW to get there Garden State Parkway, exit 117, to Route 36 East. Follow signs to Sandy Hook. Just before Sandy Hook is Atlantic Highlands. Left on First Avenue in Atlantic Highlands to Municipal Harbor Parking Area.

SANDY HOOK BAY

Atlantic Highlands Pier

Municipal Harbor Parking Area

Simon Lake Dr.

★ START

Ocean Blvd. (Scenic Dr.)

First Ave.

Hofbrauhaus

E. Highlands Rd.

36

36W

Valley Rd.

Navesink Ave.

Mt. Mitchill Scenic Overlook

NORTH

Highlands Hilltopper: Directions at a Glance

1. Parking area to Simon Lake Drive. Simon Lake Drive becomes First Avenue.
2. First Avenue to Ocean Boulevard (Scenic Drive). Left onto Ocean Boulevard.
3. Bear left at East Highlands Road fork.
4. Ocean Boulevard to Mt. Mitchill Scenic Overlook.
5. U-turn at Mt. Mitchill.
6. Left at Mt. Mitchill entrance/exit stop sign.
7. Right at next stop sign.
8. Cross over Route 36 to Navesink Road.
9. Bear right onto Valley Drive.
10. Bear left at Route 36 (Memorial Parkway) intersection.
11. Right onto First Avenue.
12. First Avenue to Municipal Harbor parking area.

Ride down First Avenue to Ocean Boulevard two hundred yards away. Make a left onto Ocean Boulevard, also known as Scenic Drive. Make your way up Ocean Boulevard. Be prepared for a long climb to the top.

Continue along Ocean Boulevard. Eventually you'll come to a fork in the road. Bear left. (If you go straight, you'll be on East Highlands Road, which is a dead end.) Continue along Ocean Boulevard until you arrive at the Hofbrauhaus Restaurant.

This is your first scenic stop. Although Mt. Mitchill is known for its wonderful views, the views of Sandy Hook and Sandy Hook Bay are actually better here than they are at Mt. Mitchill, your next stop. On a clear day, it is even possible to see the lower part of the New York skyline.

Continue along Ocean Boulevard until you reach the entrance to Mt. Mitchill Scenic Overlook, part of the Monmouth County Parks System. Mt. Mitchill is the highest point on the Eastern Seaboard; it rises 266 feet above sea level. Once again you'll enjoy a grand sight of

Sandy Hook and its bay, provided that the park's attendants have cleared brush and tree limbs that frequently hamper the view.

Turn around and return to Mt. Mitchill Scenic Overlook entrance/exit. There is a stop sign here. Make a left. Ride down the small hill to the next stop sign. This time make a right and ride to the Route 36 traffic light. Signs will point to Red Bank. Cross over Route 36. You'll now be on Navesink Avenue, also called Route 8B. On your left you'll pass Hartshorne Woods Park.

Continue on Navesink Avenue to the intersection where Locust Avenue, Monmouth Avenue, and Valley Drive (also called Route 8A) meet. Bear right and proceed on Valley Drive.

A mile or so up the road is the Route 36 intersection. Bear left onto Route 36 (Memorial Parkway), but do so with caution. This is a major thoroughfare. It is the only way, however, to get back to the downtown area of Atlantic Highlands and the Municipal Harbor parking area where the tour began.

Proceed on Route 36 West to the traffic light at the First Avenue intersection. Make a right onto First Avenue and ride to the end of it where the Municipal Harbor parking area is located. This is the end of the tour.

Navesink River Ramble

County:	Monmouth
Number of Miles:	11.7
Degree of Difficulty:	Moderate
Terrain:	Some hills
Surface:	Mostly good
Things to See:	Navesink River, Locust, British Retreat Route of 1778

The town of Rumson and the Navesink River area of Middletown are two of the prettiest, and wealthiest, parts of the North Jersey Shore; million-dollar mansions are not uncommon. The close proximity to New York and the industrial centers of North Jersey as well as the Shore's beach and boating areas make this an ideal place to live—if you can afford it.

Happily, it costs nothing to ride through this picturesque area on your bicycle. The tour commences at the intersection of Bingham Avenue and River Road in Rumson. Bingham Avenue is also known as Route 8A. Head north on Route 8A toward the river. Just prior to the Oceanic Bridge, which spans the Navesink River, you'll pass the Fisherman's Wharf Restaurant on your left. Ride over the Oceanic Bridge. To your right is the Navesink's outlet to Sandy Hook Bay.

Once you're off the bridge, you'll round the bend that hugs the Navesink River and make a right at the intersection. This is still Route 8A, but now you're in Locust, not Rumson. Locust is a historic district of Middletown. It was settled in the late eighteenth century. Originally, it was an oyster and shellfish village, but over the years it became a summer resort for New York artists and theater performers.

Make a right onto Locust Avenue, which is a continuation of

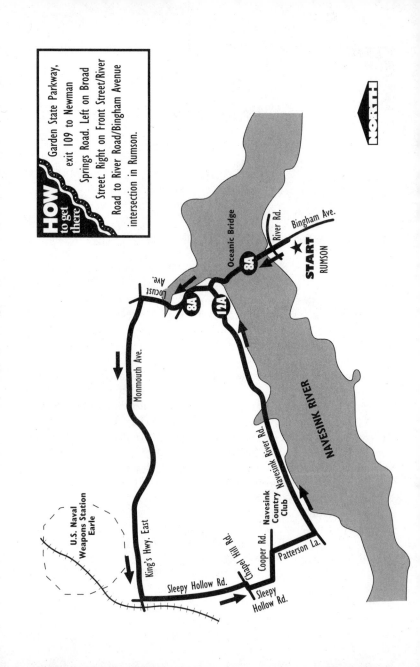

NORTH

HOW to get there

Garden State Parkway, exit 109 to Newman Springs Road. Left on Broad Street. Right on Front Street/River Road to River River Road/Bingham Avenue intersection in Rumson.

Oceanic Bridge

River Rd.

Bingham Ave.

8A

8A

START RUMSON

Locust Ave.

8A

12A

Monmouth Ave.

NAVESINK RIVER

Navesink River Rd.

Navesink Country Club

King's Hwy. East

U.S. Naval Weapons Station Earle

Cooper Rd.

Chapel Hill Rd.

Patterson La.

Sleepy Hollow Rd.

Sleepy Hollow Rd.

Navesink River Ramble: Directions at a Glance

1. Route 8A, over Oceanic Bridge.
2. Right at intersection (still Route 8A).
3. Right onto Locust Avenue.
4. Left onto Monmouth Avenue/King's Highway East.
5. Left onto Sleepy Hollow Road.
6. Right onto Chapel Hill Road.
7. Left back onto Sleepy Hollow Road.
8. Left onto Cooper Road.
9. Right onto Patterson Lane.
10. Left onto Navesink River Road (Route 12A).
11. Right onto Route 8A, back over Oceanic Bridge.

Route 8A. Cross over the small bridge, and at the intersection of Routes 8A and 8B, make a left onto Monmouth Avenue, which later turns into King's Highway East. It was here that British forces, fleeing the Continental Army of General George Washington after the Battle of Monmouth in June 1778 (see Monmouth Battlefield tour), camped while waiting for boats to arrive at nearby Sandy Hook. From Sandy Hook the British escaped to New York, thanks to the help of local Tories. This road was also a common trail (the Minnisink Trail) used by local Indians.

Proceed on Monmouth Avenue/King's Highway East. You'll notice that the old properties found in Locust gradually give way to new homes and developments located in the Chapel Hill section of Middletown. In earlier times most of the land on which the newer homes now stand were grazing pastures and part of the many horse farms that dotted Middletown.

At the King's Highway/Sleepy Hollow Road traffic light intersection, make a left onto Sleepy Hollow Road. You'll notice on your right signs that state: U.S. GOVERNMENT PROPERTY. NO TRESPASSING. Behind the fence is a skinny stretch of property on which is located a military-only railroad. The railroad connects two sections of the U.S. Naval Weapons Station at Earle.

At the "T" intersection and stop sign, make a right onto Chapel Hill Road and then a fast left back onto another section of Sleepy Hollow Road. You'll come to another "T" intersection and another stop sign. Make a left here onto Cooper Road. Three streets later, make a right onto Patterson Lane.

Patterson Lane isn't paved, but it is usually kept in good condition. It's only a short distance that you'll have to ride on Patterson Lane, anyway. At the end of it, you'll come to yet another "T" intersection and stop sign. Make a left onto Navesink River Road, also called Route 12A.

Navesink River Road is certainly the most scenic road on this tour. Be prepared for some hills, though. To your right is the Navesink River, and all around you are million-dollar properties. You'll pass the Navesink Country Club and its golf course on your left and delightful views of the river on your right.

Continue on Navesink River Road (Route 12A) to the blinking light about three miles or so down the road. At the blinking light make a right back onto Route 8A. Round the bend and go back over the Oceanic Bridge to your starting point in Rumson at the corner of Route 8A (Bingham Avenue) and River Road. The tour concludes here.

Holmdel Hustle

County:	Monmouth
Number of Miles:	12.9
Degree of Difficulty:	Moderate to difficult
Terrain:	Hilly
Surface:	Good
Things to See:	Tatum Park, Holmes–Hendrickson House, Holmdel Park, Longstreet Farm

Holmdel is a large, semirural community located in upper Monmouth County. Home of the Garden State Arts Center, Bell Labs, sprawling parks, million-dollar homes, and long, winding country roads, Holmdel can be a bicyclist's delight. The Garden State Parkway cuts right through the center of Holmdel; thus, the township and the tour of it described below are easily accessible for those arriving by car.

Although the roads on this tour are in a semirural setting, they are not free of traffic. Holmdel is a growing community, and development is in full stride. Therefore, be certain to abide by the rules of the road and ride with caution. Some roads on this tour do not have standard shoulders, so stay as far to the right as possible, especially when negotiating bends and turns where you might not be visible to approaching vehicles.

The tour begins in the parking lot of the Special Services Section of Tatum Park, located off Holland Road. Proceed out of the parking lot and turn left onto Holland Road. Pass through the traffic light at the intersection of Holland Road and Van Schoick Road, and continue on Holland to South Holland Road about a mile away.

Make a left onto South Holland Road. A half mile down South Holland Road, you'll cross underneath the Garden State Parkway.

There is a "T" intersection at the end of South Holland Road.

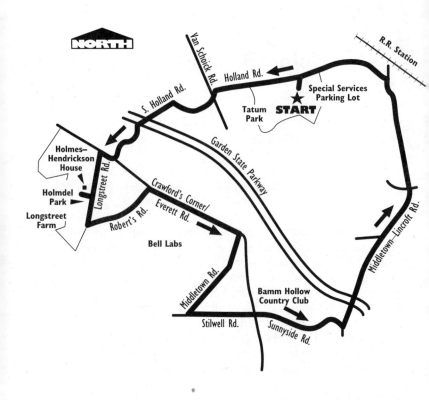

NORTH

Van Schoick Rd.

R.R. Station

Holland Rd.

S. Holland Rd.

Special Services
Parking Lot

Tatum
Park

START

Garden State Parkway

Holmes–
Hendrickson
House

Longstreet Rd.

Crawford's Corner/
Everett Rd.

Holmdel
Park

Longstreet
Farm

Robert's Rd.

Bell Labs

Middletown–Lincroft Rd.

Middletown Rd.

Bamm Hollow
Country Club

Stilwell Rd.

Sunnyside Rd.

HOW
to get
there

Garden State Parkway, exit 114, Red Hill Road to Van Schoick
Road. Right on Holland Road to entrance of Special Services Section
of Tatum Park.

Holmdel Hustle: Directions at a Glance

1. Left onto Holland Road.
2. Left onto South Holland Road.
3. Right onto Crawford's Corner/Everett Road.
4. Left onto Longstreet Road.
5. Left onto Robert's Road.
6. Right onto Crawford's Corner/Everett Road.
7. Right onto Middletown Road.
8. Left onto Stilwell Road.
9. Left onto Middletown–Lincroft Road.
10. Left onto Holland Road.
11. Left into entrance of Special Services Section of Tatum Park.

Make a right onto Crawford's Corner/Everett Road. Proceed a short distance, perhaps 300 yards or so, to the Longstreet Road traffic light. Make a left onto Longstreet Road. A quarter mile from the traffic light, you'll pass the Holmdel Activity Center on your right. Farther down the road, also on your right and just prior to Holmdel Park, is the Holmes–Hendrickson House, your first stop.

This restored Dutch-English house, built in 1754, is open to the public, but on a limited basis. Guides are there June through October, but only four days a week. (Call 908–462–1466 for details.)

In the Holmes–Hendrickson House are colonial kitchen displays, antique furniture, and farm tools. The guide will explain to you the history of the house and its importance in depicting the integration of Dutch and English customs by colonists.

Immediately after the Holmes–Hendrickson House is the entrance to Holmdel Park and Longstreet Farm. Be certain to allow some time here. Longstreet Farm is a working, "living history" farm, one that was prosperous from the mid-1700s to the 1920s and was owned by one of the first Dutch families to settle in Monmouth County. Today, Longstreet Farm is maintained by the Monmouth County Parks Commission.

In the various barns and farm buildings, you'll view turn-of-the-century farm machines and Victorian carriages. Park employees dressed in Victorian garb perform routine farm chores the same way they were performed one hundred years ago.

Do be sure to tour the Longstreet Farm farmhouse, which has been restored and is decorated in delightful Victorian style. The last of the Longstreets were gentlemen farmers, and their wealth is evident here.

After your visit to Holmdel Park's Longstreet Farm, ride out the park's exit and back onto Longstreet Road. Ride to the intersection of Longstreet Road and Robert's Road. Make a left onto Robert's Road and ride to the Crawford's Corner/Everett Road intersection. Make a right onto Crawford's Corner/Everett Road.

Proceed on Crawford's Corner/Everett Road. On your right is the huge Bell Labs complex. Near the Bell Labs tower you'll find a plaque that commemorates the discovery of radio-like waves from outer space by Bell Labs scientist Karl Jansky in 1982. The discovery began the science of radio astronomy.

At the traffic light, make a right onto Middletown Road. (The road to the left of the light, opposite Middletown Road, is called Red Hill Road.) Proceed through to the traffic light at the American Way intersection, continuing on Middletown Road. Make a left onto Stilwell Road, a picturesque country lane.

Proceed to the Crawford's Corner/Everett Road intersection. (You have completed a loop; that's why you're back at Crawford's Corner/Everett Road.) Cross over Crawford's Corner/Everett Road. Stilwell Road now becomes Sunnyside Road. On both sides of the road is the Bamm Hollow Country Club.

At the Middletown–Lincroft Road intersection there is a stop sign. Make a left here onto Middletown–Lincroft Road. Once again, you'll pass under the Garden State Parkway, a short distance up the road. Proceed through the traffic light at Dwight Road/Nut Swamp Road and Middletown-Lincroft Road. This is the route British soldiers under General Sir Henry Clinton used to make their retreat from Washington's Continental forces after the Battle of Monmouth in June 1778 (see Monmouth Battlefield tour). The British ultimately made it to Sandy Hook, where they boarded boats and crossed lower New York Harbor to Manhattan and safety.

Pass through the Bamm Hollow/Oak Hill Road and Middletown–Lincroft Road intersection, where another traffic light is located. Continue on Middletown–Lincroft Road. Pass the Middletown Railroad Station on your right. Immediately after the station, make a left onto Holland Road. If you come to the railroad tracks that cut across Middletown–Lincroft Road, you missed the left turn onto Holland Road.

Pass through the stop sign intersection at at Holland and Red Hill Road. Continue on Holland to the entrance of the Special Services Section of Tatum Park, the tour's starting point. Make a left into Tatum Park and proceed to the parking lot.

Monmouth Battlefield

County:	Monmouth
Number of Miles:	8.7
Degree of Difficulty:	Easy
Terrain:	Flat
Surface:	Good
Things to See:	Monmouth Battlefield State Park, Visitor's Center, Battleview Orchards, Molly Pitcher's Well, Owl Haven Nature Center, Old Tennent Church

The Battle of Monmouth was a crucial Revolutionary War engagement fought between General George Washington's Continental Army and British regulars. It occurred on June 28, 1778. Washington's victory at Monmouth enabled him to rally the American forces and fellow patriots after a brutal, demoralizing winter spent at Valley Forge.

Much of the battlefield is now part of Monmouth Battlefield State Park. Located in Freehold on Route 33, just beyond the Route 33–Route 9 junction (formerly the Freehold Circle), the park is well worth a visit. To explore it and its surrounding points of interest by bicycle is the most rewarding way to step back into history.

Before you do any cycling, be certain first to spend some time in the Monmouth Battlefield State Park Visitor's Center. Since Monmouth Battlefield is one of New Jersey's newest state parks, the facilities are modern and the displays are both interesting and informative. A large electronic map tells the story of the strategies and troop movements during this pivotal battle and should be your first stop. There is also a small gift stand where visitors can purchase souvenirs and additional material on the battle as well as pick up free park maps and brochures.

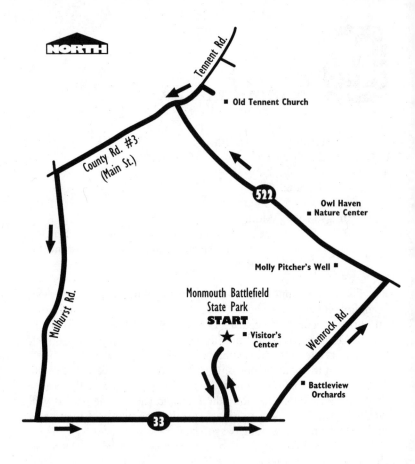

NORTH

Tennent Rd.

■ Old Tennent Church

County Rd. #3
(Main St.)

522

Owl Haven
■ Nature Center

Molly Pitcher's Well ■

Monmouth Battlefield
State Park
START

★ ■ Visitor's
Center

Mulhurst Rd.

Wemrock Rd.

■ Battleview
Orchards

33

HOW
to get
there
Route 9 to Route 33 West
to the entrance of Monmouth
Battlefield State Park.

Monmouth Battlefield: Directions at a Glance

1. Out Monmouth Battlefield State Park and left onto Route 33.
2. Left onto Wemrock Road.
3. Left onto Route 522.
4. Right onto Tennent Road. Visit Old Tennent Church.
5. Return to Tennent Road. Cross over Route 522. Tennent Road becomes Main Street (County Road #3). Proceed on Main Street.
6. Left onto Millhurst Road.
7. Left onto Route 33.
8. Left back into Monmouth Battlefield State Park. Ride to Visitor's Center parking lot.

Monmouth Battlefield has hiking trails and limited bicycle paths within the park boundaries. Cyclists can spend a good part of a morning leisurely riding the park trail network, so do bring lunch if you plan to spend the day. Use one of the free park maps available at the Visitor's Center to plan your ride within the park.

The Monmouth Battlefield tour described below deals mostly with the roads and things to see just outside the park. Perhaps the best way to enjoy the Monmouth Battlefield experience on bike is to arrive early in the morning, spend some time at the Visitor's Center, ride the park's paths, have a picnic lunch, and then ride the tour described below.

Park your car in the Visitor's Center parking lot. Follow the exit signs out of the park. At the park's entrance/exit, make a left onto Route 33. Be advised that this is a heavy-use road, so proceed with caution. Make a left at the traffic light onto Wemrock Road.

A short distance form this intersection is Battleview Orchards, a popular apple, peach, and pumpkin "pick-your-own" farm. You can also purchase some of New Jersey's finest apple cider here in the fall as well as apple pies, apple cider donuts, and Battleview jam and jelly.

Proceed on Wemrock Road after your stop at Battleview Orchards. You'll pass Battleview's apple orchards and the remains of an old farm on your left. At the stop sign, which is the intersection of Wemrock Road and Route 522, make a left. Once again, ride with caution, since this is a frequently traveled road.

Approximately an eighth of a mile from the Wemrock Road/Route 522 intersection on the left side of the road is the famous Molly Pitcher's Well. It was Molly Pitcher, according to legend, who gave water to thirsty patriots during the Battle of Monmouth. And when her husband was wounded, Molly took his place beside his cannon. Because of her valor, it is said Molly Pitcher was made an honorary officer in the Continental Army.

Be advised that the well on Route 522, although called Molly Pitcher's Well and celebrated as such, is not, say historians, the actual well where Molly Pitcher drew water during the Battle of Monmouth. That well, as the plaque on Route 522 will tell you, is located some 200 yards to the east.

Your next stop on Route 522 is the Owl Haven Nature Center. It is located about half a mile from Molly Pitcher's Well on the right side of the road. Run by the New Jersey Audubon Society, Owl Haven contains numerous environmental exhibits. It's worth a stop.

Leave the Owl Haven Nature Center parking lot and continue west on Route 522. At the traffic light, which is the intersection of Route 522 and Tennent Road, make a right and ride to the Old Tennent Church. It's located a few hundred yards from the intersection on your right. It was here that a hospital was set up to care for the American wounded during the Battle of Monmouth. In the cemetery that surrounds the front and sides of the church are the remains of American and British soldiers killed in the battle.

Go back to the traffic light at the Route 522 and Tennent Road intersection. Just beyond the light, Tennent Road becomes Main Street, or County Road #3. Proceed down this road to the Millhurst Road (Route 527) intersection. Make a left onto Millhurst Road. Proceed south to the Route 33 intersection.

Make sure you keep to your right just after you turn left at the intersection, It will seem as if you are pedaling onto a major highway, given the nature of the entrance onto Route 33. Proceed with caution, since there are no shoulders on the long entrance ramp. Once you're off the ramp, however (it's about a half mile or so), and actually on the main section of Route 33, you will be able to cycle within a wide shoulder area back to the Monmouth Battlefield State Park entrance.

Once inside the park, proceed to the Visitor's Center parking lot, where the tour concludes.

Allaire

County:	Monmouth
Number of Miles:	8.8
Degree of Difficulty:	Easy
Terrain:	Flat
Surface:	Mostly good
Things to See:	Allaire State Park, Deserted Village, Pine Creek Railroad

Allaire State Park is yet another one of those state parks that you will want to spend some time in, either before or after you complete this bicycle tour. There is much to see and do here. Although the tour begins and ends in the park, virtually all of the tour is on roads outside it. Even though Allaire offers many activities to the park visitor, bicycling, unfortunately, isn't one of them. There are few paths or designated bike routes in the park.

But just outside Allaire is a good network of roads that wind through parts of lower Monmouth County. In order to make Allaire the starting and stopping points on the tour, I selected roads that form a loop around the park. I suggest that you arrive at Allaire early, complete your bike tour, and then spend the remainder of the day strolling about Allaire's Deserted Village and enjoying the park's other attractions. Any season except winter is a good one to visit Allaire.

Back in the early 1800s Allaire was a profitable iron ore community. Its big furnaces and the craftsmen who lived and worked in the village turned out such useful household iron products as cauldrons, pots, kettles, stoves, and piping. More than 450 people lived and worked at Allaire during the community's peak years, which were in the 1820s and 1830s.

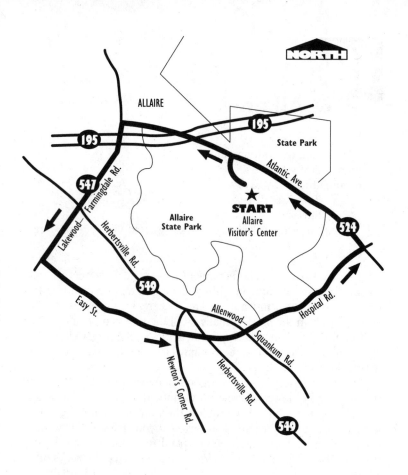

NORTH

ALLAIRE

195

195

State Park

547

Farmingdale Rd.

Atlantic Ave.

Lakewood

Herbertsville Rd.

Allaire State Park

★ **START** Allaire Visitor's Center

524

549

Easy St.

Allenwood

Squankum Rd.

Hospital Rd.

Newton's Corner Rd.

Herbertsville Rd.

549

HOW to get there — Garden State Parkway, exit 98 to Route 34 South, to Allenwood Road, to Route 524 West. Left into Allaire State Park.

Allaire: Directions at a Glance

1. Leaving Allaire State Park, left onto Route 524 (Atlantic Avenue).
2. Left onto Route 547 (Lakewood–Farmingdale Road).
3. Left onto Easy Street (Easy Street becomes Hospital Road).
4. Left onto Route 524 (Atlantic Avenue).
5. Left back into Allaire State Park.

Actually, Allaire thrived until 1846. It was in this year that coal was discovered in Pennsylvania's Allegheny Mountains. Bog iron foundries such as Allaire and Batsto, located farther south in the heart of the Pine Barrens (see The Pine Barrens tour), burned charcoal from pitch pine in their huge furnaces. But it was quickly learned that coal was cheaper to burn than charcoal. As a result, in only a few years, Allaire Village became known as the Deserted Village.

Fortunately, much of the village has been restored. And today you can wander back into history and gain a good understanding of what living and working in a nineteenth-century bog-iron community was like. In the village you can, for instance, visit the blacksmith shop, general store, and chapel. Nearby are hiking and nature trails and a picnic area.

Adjacent to the village are the Pine Creek Railroad and the Pine Creek Rail Museum. Take a ride on the railroad and its antique railcars. You can also launch a canoe on the Manasquan River in Allaire, fish, or go deer hunting during hunting season.

During spring, summer, and fall, weekends at Allaire almost always feature a special event or two. Flea markets, antique shows, craft fairs, and art exhibits are common. Camping and horseback riding are also popular at Allaire. Call (908) 938–2371 or (908) 938–2253 for a schedule of events.

To start the bicycle tour, park your car in the parking lot opposite the Pine Creek Railroad and in front of the Allaire Visitor's Center. Pedal out the park's exit to Route 524. Make a left onto Route 524, which is also known as Atlantic Avenue. A mile up Route 524, you'll pass the entrance to the Allaire State Park campgrounds.

At the traffic light, which is at the Route 524/Route 547 intersection, make a left. This is a fairly busy intersection because just down the road on Route 547 (also called Lakewood–Farmingdale Road) is an entrance to a major highway, Route 195. Proceed with caution. Bear to your left and follow signs for Route 547 South. Pass through the Herbertsville Road traffic light. The next left you can make will be onto Easy Street. Turn here. On Easy Street you'll pass small horse and chicken farms. Years ago this entire area consisted of nothing but farms. But Monmouth County has experienced a tremendous growth spurt in the last twenty years, and farmland is rapidly disappearing.

You'll pass through three stop signs before Easy Street becomes Hospital Road. The first stop sign is at the Newton's Corner intersection. The second is at the Herbertsville Road intersection. And the third is at the Squankum Road intersection. All of these occur in rather quick succession; it's barely a half mile from the first to the last stop sign.

Proceed on what is now Hospital Road. Allaire State Park property is on both sides of the road. At the next stop sign, which is located at the Hospital Road/Route 524 (Atlantic Avenue) intersection, make a left. You'll pass the Spring Meadow Golf Course, a state-owned golf course. Continue on Route 524 (Atlantic Avenue) to the entrance of Allaire State Park. Ride with caution; Route 524 is a busy road on weekends.

Make a left at the entrance to Allaire State Park and ride back to the main parking lot. The tour concludes here.

Sandy Hook

County:	Monmouth
Number of Miles:	10.6
Degree of Difficulty:	Easy
Terrain:	Flat
Surface:	Good
Things to See:	Spermaceti Visitor's Center, Atlantic Ocean, Sandy Hook Bay, Old Dune Trail, Sandy Hook Lighthouse, Fort Hancock, Sandy Hook Museum, Halyburton Monument, salt marsh

Sandy Hook is the New Jersey unit of Gateway National Recreation Area. A skinny, shifting, sand spit peninsula on the uppermost reach of the Jersey Shore, Sandy Hook offers a variety of attractions and pleasant cycling. If possible, plan to spend a full day here.

If you cycle onto Sandy Hook, you will be allowed into the park free. If you drive a vehicle in, however, you will be charged an admission fee during the park's busy months. If you drive, arrive early during the summer months and on weekends. Sandy Hook fills up quickly; once the parking lots are full, rangers close the park to vehicles.

Park your car in one of the lots just beyond the entrance to Sandy Hook. Start your tour of the Hook by exiting the parking area and making a right onto Hartshorne Drive, Sandy Hook's main thoroughfare. On your right, just beyond the seawall, is the Atlantic Ocean. To your left is Sandy Hook Bay.

It is approximately two miles to the Spermaceti Visitor's Center. Stop here to check out the exhibits and displays that pertain to Sandy Hook's natural history and former military importance. There are also

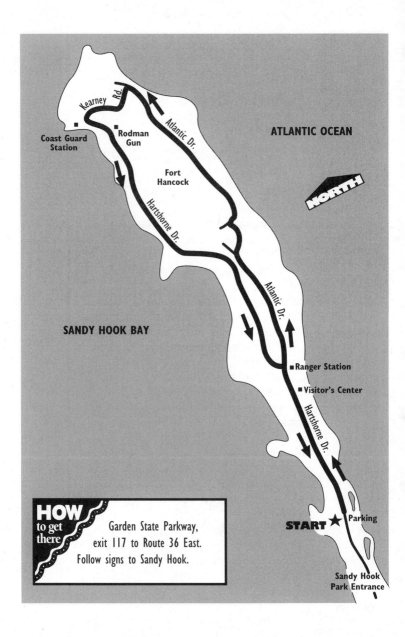

ATLANTIC OCEAN

Kearney Rd.

Atlantic Dr.

Coast Guard Station

■ Rodman Gun

Fort Hancock

Hartshorne Dr.

NORTH

Atlantic Dr.

SANDY HOOK BAY

■ **Ranger Station**

■ **Visitor's Center**

Hartshorne Dr.

HOW to get there   Garden State Parkway, exit 117 to Route 36 East. Follow signs to Sandy Hook.

START ★ Parking

Sandy Hook Park Entrance

Sandy Hook: Directions at a Glance

1. Right out of parking lot just beyond entrance to Sandy Hook onto Hartshorne Drive.
2. Visit Spermaceti Visitor's Center. Right out of parking area onto Hartshorne Drive.
3. Right onto Atlantic Drive.
4. Right at intersection just beyond bathing area (staying on Atlantic Drive).
5. Left at "T" intersection.
6. Right at first stop sign.
7. Left at second stop sign onto Kearney Road.
8. Pass Rodman Gun; visit Fort Hancock.
9. Return to Hartshorne Drive; bear right at Nike missile intersection.
10. Ride south on Hartshorne Drive to Sandy Hook's park's entrance/exit.

displays of old lifesaving apparatus. Take a few of the free brochures available at the Ranger's desk. These little pamphlets will enlighten you on Sandy Hook's delicate ecological makeup and provide historical background on Fort Hancock, which you'll visit up ahead. Such information will make your bike tour all the more rewarding.

Just beyond the parking area of the Spermaceti Visitor's Center is the Old Dune Trail, a one-mile loop that provides a good introduction to the Sandy Hook landscape. If you decide to walk it, stay on the trail. Poison ivy abounds. Keep an eye out for the many birds that use Sandy Hook as a respite, since the peninsula sits on the Atlantic Flyway. In addition to sighting common shorebirds, you might also catch a glimpse of an osprey, a yellow-bellied sapsucker, or a red-headed woodpecker.

Exit the parking area of the Spermaceti Visitor's Center and make a right back onto Hartshorne Drive. Continue to the Hartshorne Drive/Atlantic Drive intersection. Bear right onto Atlantic Drive and

head toward Gunnison and North Beaches. Along the way you'll see various shrubs, trees, and barrier beach plants indigenous to Sandy Hook.

Continue on Atlantic Drive; you'll eventually come to a bend in the road. Bear right, staying on Atlantic Drive. Up ahead you'll pass a swimming area on your right. At the next intersection, make a right and head toward North Beach. (At last look, there was no street sign at this intersection; however, park maps indicate that if you turn right, you're still on Atlantic Drive.)

Continue on Atlantic Drive. At the "T" intersection, make a left. About 150 yards away, you'll come to a stop sign. Make a right. Go to the next stop sign, about 300 yards away. In front of you will be the Sandy Hook Coast Guard Station. Make a left onto Kearney Road. Up ahead is the Fort Hancock section of Sandy Hook. On your right is Sandy Hook Bay. If you look out into the bay, you'll probably see large naval warships and supply ships at the Earle Naval Center dock, a few miles away.

On your left you'll soon approach the Rodman Gun, a huge Civil War–era cannon that is a Sandy Hook landmark. It is one of only two that still exist today. Once you pass the Rodman Gun, you are back on the main loop road in Sandy Hook—Hartshorne Drive. Here, however, Hartshorne Drive is often called "Officer's Row" because the brick buildings up ahead on your left that look out onto Sandy Hook Bay once housed the officers of Fort Hancock, an important part of America's coastal defense during World War II. Fort Hancock protected the entrance to New York Harbor.

At this point in the Sandy Hook tour, you might want to lock up your bike and walk around Fort Hancock. You can visit the Sandy Hook Museum, which contains exhibits, maps, and memorabilia that pertain to Fort Hancock's interesting history. You can also visit the Sandy Hook Lighthouse. Built in 1764, it is America's oldest operating lighthouse. On weekends in the summer and early fall, Sandy Hook often sponsors special events on the Pershing Parade Field, including music festivals and ecological fairs. Check with park rangers in advance to see what event, if any, is scheduled for the day you visit Sandy Hook.

After you finish your walking tour of Fort Hancock, return to Hartshorne Drive and proceed with your bike tour of Sandy Hook. Head south on Hartshorne Drive; again, Sandy Hook Bay will be on your right. You'll come to a yield sign intersection a half mile or so down Hartshorne Drive, where you'll bear right and exit Fort Hancock. On your left, notice the replica of the Nike missile. During the early stages of the Cold War, Fort Hancock was a strategic air defense post, serving New York and New Jersey.

Continue on Hartshorne Drive. About a mile and a half from the Fort Hancock exit you'll pass the Halyburton Monument, where excavators found the remains of British sailors from the Revolutionary War. Continue south on Hartshorne Drive. The salt marshes of Sandy Hook Bay and a good view of the Highlands will be on your right. The fortlike structure found at the very top of the Highlands is the Twin Lights Historical Site, one of America's most unusual lighthouses and the home of an excellent museum.

Continue south on Hartshorne Drive until you reach the entrance/exit of Sandy Hook, the tour's starting point.

The Barnegat Peninsula

County:	Ocean
Number of Miles:	25
Degree of Difficulty:	Easy
Terrain:	Flat
Surface:	Good
Things to See:	Manasquan Inlet, Point Pleasant Beach fishing fleet, Jersey Shore resort towns of Bay Head and Mantoloking, Barnegat Bay

The Barnegat Peninsula extends from Point Pleasant Beach all the way down to the southern tip of Island Beach State Park. This long, narrow stretch of coast *used* to be a peninsula—before the Point Pleasant Canal was dug, linking the Manasquan River with Barnegat Bay. Technically, the peninsula is now an island, although few people actually call it that. But with the Atlantic Ocean on its east side; the bay, river, and canal on its west side; and the Manasquan and Barnegat inlets forming its northern and southern boundaries, respectively, the Barnegat Peninsula literally is surrounded by water.

This tour is an early-morning-summer or weekend-in-September tour. The resort towns that line the peninsula, from Point Pleasant Beach to Seaside Park, are alive with activity and vacationers from June through August. Needless to say, vehicle and pedestrian traffic gets heavy during the day as families make their way to the beaches and boardwalks that the Barnegat Peninsula is noted for.

Traffic on the Barnegat Peninsula is lightest in early morning. The wind is still then, too, and the sun does not reach its most potent position in the sky until noon.

The tour commences in the parking lot that runs along the Point

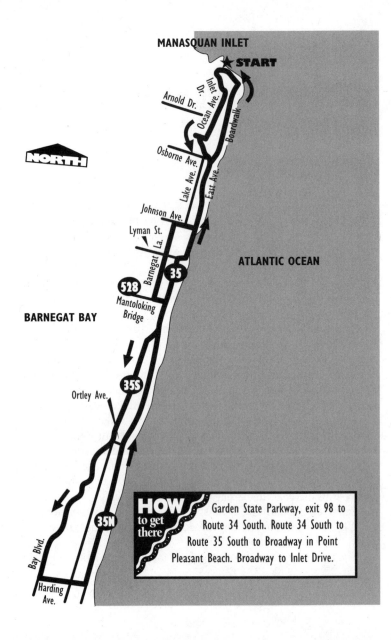

MANASQUAN INLET

★ START

Arnold Dr.

Inlet Dr.

Ocean Ave.

Boardwalk

NORTH

Osborne Ave.

Lake Ave.

East Ave.

Johnson Ave.

Lyman St.

La.

Barnegat La.

ATLANTIC OCEAN

35

528

Mantoloking Bridge

BARNEGAT BAY

35S

Ortley Ave.

35N

Bay Blvd.

Harding Ave.

HOW to get there

Garden State Parkway, exit 98 to Route 34 South. Route 34 South to Route 35 South to Broadway in Point Pleasant Beach. Broadway to Inlet Drive.

The Barnegat Peninsula: Directions at a Glance

1. Right out of Manasquan Inlet parking lot onto Inlet Drive.
2. Left at the stop sign and immediately bear right onto Ocean Avenue.
3. Proceed down Ocean Avenue through Point Pleasant Beach to Bay Head boundary traffic light (where Ocean Avenue meets Route 35). Left onto Route 35.
4. Left at next traffic light (Osborne Avenue) onto East Avenue.
5. East Avenue to its conclusion at Lyman Street.
6. Right on Lyman, then left onto Route 35 South.
7. Route 35 South, past the start of the divided highway (Route 35 divides into separate north and south lanes).
8. Right onto Ortley Avenue in Lavallette, then turn left onto Bay Boulevard.
9. Bay Boulevard to Harding Avenue. Make left onto Harding.
10. Cross over Route 35 South. Left onto Route 35 North.
11. North on Route 35 through Lavallette, Ocean Beach, Normandy Beach and into Mantoloking.
12. Left at Mantoloking Bridge traffic light (Route 528).
13. Right onto Barnegat Lane (becomes Clayton Avenue in Bay Head).
14. Bear right onto Johnson Avenue at conclusion of Barnegat Lane. Turn left onto Lake Avenue in Bay Head.
15. Left onto Lake Avenue to Osborne Avenue. Make a right, then a left onto Route 35 North.
16. Bear right at next traffic light onto Ocean Avenue.
17. Ocean Avenue to Inlet Drive and Manasquan Inlet parking lot.

Pleasant Beach section of the Manasquan Inlet. To park here, you must arrive early. The inlet is a popular fishing spot, and anglers are usually early risers. If there are no spaces left, you can park in Jenkinson's parking lot, which is adjacent to the inlet parking lot. There is a fee to park in Jenkinson's.

Make a right out of whichever lot you find a space in and ride around the U-shaped Inlet Drive. You'll pass the Manasquan Inlet Coast Guard Station and Point Pleasant Beach's commercial fishing fleet. At the stop sign, make a left and immediately bear right onto Ocean Avenue. There are no shoulders on Ocean Avenue and plenty of parked cars in the summer. Ride with caution. Once you pass the Arnold Avenue traffic light about a mile away, Ocean Avenue becomes less congested. At that point you'll also get a glimpse of Point Pleasant Beach's boardwalk and amusement rides.

Continue on Ocean Avenue until the end of Point Pleasant Beach and the beginning of Bay Head, one of the Shore's prettiest resort towns. At the "T" intersection traffic light where Ocean Avenue meets Route 35, make a left. Follow signs for Bay Head, Mantoloking, and Seaside Heights. At the next traffic light, some two hundred yards away, make a left onto Osborne Avenue, which quickly leads you onto East Avenue.

Proceed down East Avenue through the towns of Bay Head and Mantoloking. You will see million-dollar mansions on the beach side of East Avenue. Once again, ride with caution. Beachgoers must cross East Avenue to get to the sand and surf.

East Avenue eventually runs into Lyman Street. Make a right onto Lyman, go one block to the Route 35 intersection, and make a left. Route 35 is the Barnegat Peninsula's main artery. Although it's a busy road, Route 35 does have shoulders suitable for cycling. Nonetheless, ride with caution.

Proceed on Route 35 South through Mantoloking and then into the southern section of the Barnegat Peninsula. You'll know you're there because Route 35 goes from two to four lanes. The two southbound lanes run parallel to Barnegat Bay, while the two northbound lanes are closer to the ocean. At that point where Route 35 divides into separate north- and southbound lanes, simply bear right and remain on Route 35 South. The shoulder will become even wider, and you'll have a great view of the bay as you pass through such small summer resort towns as Normandy and Ocean Beaches, Lavallette, and finally Ortley Beach.

Stay on Route 35 South until you enter the town of Lavallette, approximately four miles from the point where Route 35 divided into separate north and south lanes. The first traffic light in Lavallette is Ortley Avenue. Make a right onto Ortley Avenue, go one block, and turn left onto Bay Boulevard. Bay Boulevard hugs Barnegat Bay and continues into the town of Ortley Beach.

Just prior to the Ortley Beach/Seaside Heights border is Harding Avenue. Make a left onto Harding. Cross over Route 35 South. A block or two later is the Route 35 North intersection. Make a left here.

You are now beginning your return trip. Expect some congestion as you ride up Route 35 North through the towns of Ortley Beach, Lavallette, and Ocean Beach. Watch out for cars pulling out of parking spaces and pedestrians heading for the beach.

Continue on Route 35 North through Normandy Beach. Pass the point where Route 35 divides into north and south lanes. Continue into Mantoloking. About a mile north of the Route 35 division is the turn for the Mantoloking Bridge (Route 528). You'll know it because it is the second traffic light after the Route 35 split. Make a left here, but do not go over the bridge. Instead, make a sudden right onto Barnegat Lane, a skinny stretch of road that runs parallel with Route 35. Continue along Barnegat Lane to its conclusion about two miles from its origin. In Bay Head, Barnegat Lane turns into Clayton Avenue. Follow the road as it bears right onto Johnson Avenue, then make your first left, which is not more than 200 feet away.

You are now on Lake Avenue. Ride up Lake Avenue and pass the picturesque side streets. You'll see why Bay Head reminds some people of Cape Cod. Its weatherworn cedar-shake beach houses seem transplanted from the windswept Cape. Pass through the Bridge Avenue intersection where Bay Head's small cluster of shops is located. Continue on Lake Avenue. On your left will be Twilight Lake. Three streets to your right is the ocean.

Lake Avenue ends at Osborne Avenue. Make a right onto Osborne and then a left at the traffic light back onto Route 35 North. At the next traffic light, approximately 200 yards away, bear right. You'll now be on Ocean Avenue in Point Pleasant Beach again. Ride up Ocean Avenue all the way back to the Manasquan Inlet, about two miles away. This concludes the tour.

Island Beach State Park

County:	Ocean
Number of Miles:	16.2
Degree of Difficulty:	Easy
Terrain:	Flat
Surface:	Good
Things to See:	Aeolium (Island Beach Nature Center), barrier beach landscape, wildlife sanctuary, Barnegat Lighthouse ("Old Barney"), Barnegat Inlet

The thin stretch of barrier beach that is Island Beach State Park is, perhaps, the prettiest part of the entire New Jersey Shore. It is made up of miles of unspoiled sandy beaches; delicate, shifting sand dunes; thickets; marshes; and a wildlife sanctuary, home to numerous species of birds including the once endangered osprey. Situated south of Seaside Park with the Atlantic Ocean on one side and Barnegat Bay on the other, Island Beach is the largest undisturbed barrier beach of its kind in New Jersey. And passing right down the center of it, like a spinal cord, is a straight, two-lane road—ideal for cycling.

It is 8.1 miles from the Island Beach State Park entrance at the end of Central Avenue in Seaside Park to where the paved park road ends. Since there is only one road, this tour is a simple down-and-back one. Still, there is much to see in the way of barrier-beach vegetation and birdlife. Do remember to pack binoculars. Island Beach State Park, like Sandy Hook to the north, is located on the Atlantic Flyway, so you'll almost always spot plenty of birds along the tour, especially in the fall.

If you decide to tour Island Beach in the summer or early fall, bring your bathing suit. There are a number of beach access paths along the tour. Feel free to break up your ride with a refreshing ocean

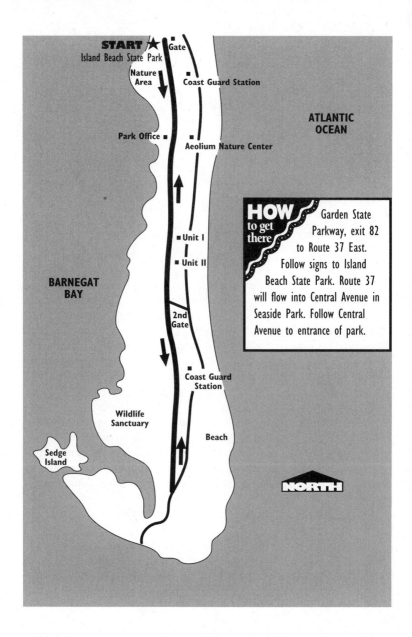

Island Beach State Park: Directions at a Glance

1. Follow the one and only park road from the entrance to the southern tip of the park and back again.

dip. Most swimming areas have showers and changing areas, so you won't have to ride in a wet swimsuit.

Island Beach State Park is divided into three zones. The northern third of the park is a state natural area. The central third is a recreation zone. And the southern third is also a natural area; it includes the park's wildlife sanctuary.

It is a little over a mile from the park's entrance to the Aeolium, or Island Beach Nature Center. Stop here to view the slide show, which will give you a brief overview of barrier beach ecology and the history of Island Beach State Park. View, too, the small nature exhibits. Also, pick up free brochures that describe vegetation you'll pass along the way and birds you might see in it or just above it.

If you have the time or inclination, walk the short nature trail that begins adjacent to the Aeolium. It offers an "on-site" opportunity to examine barrier beach vegetation up close. But be forewarned. Poison ivy is common at Island Beach, and the mosquitos can be bothersome.

After visiting the Aeolium, continue riding south into the park. The bike path/shoulder you're on, though, ends three miles later. Those who prefer not to ride to the end of the paved road should turn around here. The total mileage for this abbreviated tour is eight miles. Those who proceed should ride to the right and obey traffic laws.

Proceed south to the end of the paved road. There are no turnoffs, bends, or shortcuts. When you arrive at your destination some four miles later, lock your bike and walk to the beach. More ambitious tourists might walk along the beach the mile and a half to Barnegat Inlet.

At one time Island Beach ended where the paved road ends, but through almost a century of currents and storms, a stretch of sand more than a mile long has built up at the southern end of the peninsula.

Just across the Inlet that separates Island Beach State Park from Long Beach Island is "Old Barney," one of the most photographed and painted lighthouses in all America. After enjoying the view, walk back to your bike and start your return journey.

Island Beach can get windy in late afternoon. Fortunately, the prevailing wind is generally southerly—which means a good tailwind for your return trip. If you have a headwind, use the drafting technique described in the "Basics of Bicycle Touring" section of this book. Of course, in order to draft you need at least two riders. If you're alone, you're out of luck.

Some other helpful hints when touring Island Beach Sate Park: If you're as much a bird-watcher as you are a bicyclist, the best time of day to tour Island Beach is early morning or dusk because park birds are most active then. Those who sunburn easily should wear sunscreen if touring in the summer. The sun can be strong, and there are few shady spots along the road. Summer weekends at Island Beach usually mean crowds and traffic. Avoid touring on Saturdays and Sundays if you can. Finally, if you plan to walk any nature trails or partake in any ranger-led activities in the brush, bring insect repellent.

Long Beach Island North Loop

County:	Ocean
Number of Miles:	18
Degree of Difficulty:	Easy
Terrain:	Flat
Surface:	Good
Things to See:	Barnegat Light Historical Museum, Barnegat Lighthouse State Park, "Old Barney" the lighthouse, Viking Village, views of Barnegat fishing fleet, Barnegat Bay and Barnegat Inlet

Long Beach Island is one of the Jersey Shore's most popular vacation spots. A skinny stretch of barrier island four miles off Ocean County's coast, Long Beach Island has beautiful beaches, rows of well-kept summer cottages, and a history that includes the settlement of New England whalers and the formation of a prosperous eighteenth-century whaling industry.

Today, Long Beach Island's main industry is summer tourism. Although there is a small year-round population on the island, the towns that make up Long Beach Island just about close up during the winter months. In the winter, cold winds blow hard and frequently, and the sea is rough and choppy. But in the summer and fall Long Beach Island is one of the best places in all of New Jersey for sun, sand, and surf.

Obviously, the best time to tour Long Beach Island is in the summer or early fall. (During the spring, the winds are still fairly strong.) Long Beach Island is eighteen miles long, from the southern tip of the Holgate Division of the Edwin B. Forsythe Wildlife Refuge Area to the northernmost point of Barnegat Lighthouse State Park. The width of the island is about a mile and a half at its widest point.

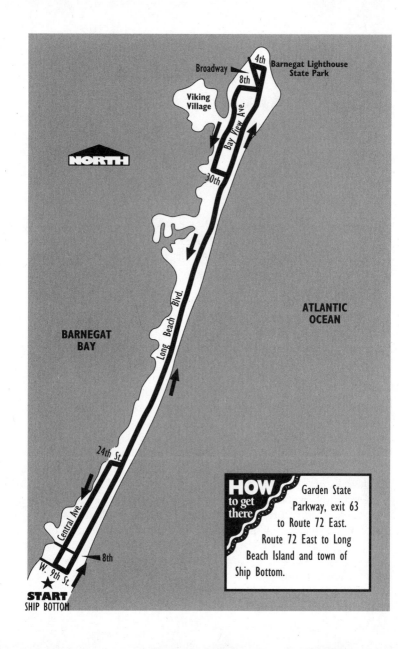

Long Beach Island North Loop: Directions at a Glance

1. North on Long Beach Boulevard from 8th Street intersection.
2. Pass through Ship Bottom, Surf City, North Beach, Harvey Cedars, Loveladies, and Barnegat Light. (Long Beach Boulevard becomes Central Avenue in Barnegat Light.)
3. Bear left onto 4th Street.
4. Right at stop sign (Broadway).
5. Right into entrance of Barnegat Lighthouse State Park.
6. Left out entrance of Barnegat Lighthouse State Park. Proceed on Broadway to 8th Street in Barnegat Light.
7. Right onto 8th Street.
8. Left onto Bay View Avenue.
9. Left onto 30th Street.
10. Right onto Long Beach Boulevard.
11. Long Beach Boulevard to intersection of 24th Street in Surf City.
12. Right onto 24th Street.
13. Left onto Central Avenue.
14. Left onto West 9th Street in Ship Bottom.
15. Left onto Long Beach Boulevard to 8th Street.

Because a grand loop tour of Long Beach Island would add up to at least thirty-six miles—hardly a "short" bike tour, especially when one takes into account the various stops and things to see—I've broken up the island tour into a North Loop and South Loop.

Both tours originate in Ship Bottom, the centermost town on Long Beach Island and the town in which the Route 72 East Causeway ends. If, however, you're vacationing on the island and wish to complete one (or both) of these tours, you can start anywhere on the loop.

During the summer, the best time to tour Long Beach Island is on a weekday. On weekends traffic is heavy. The tour roads are wide, however, and there are well-maintained shoulders on most of them, so if you do choose a weekend to tour the island, you'll still be able to enjoy your ride.

The North Loop tour begins at the intersection of 8th Street and Long Beach Boulevard in Ship Bottom. Eighth Street runs widthwise and connects with the Route 72 Causeway, a half mile away. Long Beach Boulevard is one of the island's main arteries. It runs the length of Long Beach Island, although it also goes by the name Bay Avenue in Beach Haven, Central Avenue in Barnegat Light, and Route 607 on official state maps.

Proceed north on Long Beach Boulevard through Ship Bottom and then Surf City. These are two densely populated beach towns in the summer, so traffic may be a bit heavy here. Beware of cars pulling in and out of parking spaces and bathers walking to and from the beach. Beyond Surf City, traffic becomes noticeably lighter.

Continue on Long Beach Boulevard through the towns of North Beach, Harvey Cedars, and Loveladies. Yes, the latter two names really are the names of these communities. Back in the 1700s there were cedar trees on this part of the island. As for "Harvey," the town was originally known as Harvey's Whaling Station. Loveladies was named after a local hunter, Thomas Lovelady.

Loveladies is known today for its outstanding collection of contemporary beach homes. Back in 1962 a severe winter storm destroyed most of Loveladies. Homes were washed away by pounding waves and flooding. Property damage ran in the millions. The devastation didn't discourage homeowners from rebuilding, however. What went up were magnificent beach homes with the latest in contemporary architectural design. And all the new homes were constructed on pilings—for protection from future storms and flooding. You'll see these homes on both sides of Long Beach Boulevard.

After Loveladies comes the town of Barnegat Light. Long Beach Boulevard becomes Central Avenue here. At the corner of 5th and Central avenues you'll come to the Barnegat Light Historical Museum, your first stop. The museum is in a former one-room schoolhouse. It contains a number of relics and old photographs from Barnegat Light's Victorian era as well as the original lens of "Old Barney," Barnegat Light's famous lighthouse and namesake, your next stop.

After visiting the museum, stroll through the Edith Duff Gwin Gardens, located behind the museum. *Note:* The museum has a limited schedule, even in the summer. Check with the Long Beach Island Information Center in Ship Bottom, (609) 499–3407, to find out what days the museum is open.

Leave the museum and continue on Central Avenue to the bend, a street away. Bear left. You're now on 4th Street. At the stop sign on Broadway, make a right. A hundred yards or so on your right is the entrance to Barnegat Lighthouse State Park, home of Old Barney, the lighthouse. In front of you is Barnegat Inlet. The land beyond the inlet is Island Beach State Park (see the Island Beach State Park tour described earlier).

It is said that Old Barney is the most photographed and painted lighthouse in America; it's one of the few that visitors are still allowed to enter. Climb to the top and you'll have a spectacular bird's-eye view of the Jersey coast.

Barnegat Lighthouse State Park is a good place to take a swim should you want to cool off. There are showers here and a place to change clothes. Other than swim and visit Old Barney, there is little to do in this, New Jersey's smallest, state park. Make a left out the entrance/exit of the park, and proceed down Broadway to 8th Street.

Make a right on 8th Street and go down to Bay View Avenue where you'll make a left. As you ride down Bay View, you'll get a good glimpse of Barnegat Light's fishing fleet and Barnegat Bay on your right. At the intersection of Bay View and 19th Street, make a right into Viking Village. In the little shacks and shanties, you'll find nautical nicknacks for sale as well as handmade gifts and paintings by local artists.

Continue on Bay View until it ends at 30th Street. Bear left here and go to the stop sign, where you'll make a right. You're now back on Long Beach Boulevard. Continue south on Long Beach Boulevard back through Loveladies, Harvey Cedars, and North Beach.

At the intersection of 24th Street and Long Beach Boulevard in Surf City, make a right. Shortly thereafter, at the yield sign, make a left onto Central Avenue (not the same Central Avenue as the one in Barnegat Light). Follow Central Avenue south toward the Route 72 Causeway.

Pass through Surf City. In Ship Bottom make a left onto West 9th Street. Ride one block and make a left onto Long Beach Boulevard to 8th Street where the tour began.

Long Beach Island
South Loop

County:	Ocean
Number of Miles:	14.1
Degree of Difficulty:	Easy
Terrain:	Flat
Surface:	Good
Things to See:	Bay Village, Fantasy Island, Surflight Theater, Long Beach Island Historical Museum

The South Loop tour of Long Beach Island takes in the bottom half of the island. You'll pass through the towns of Ship Bottom, Brant Beach, and Beach Haven. Unlike the North Loop tour, you won't ride to the tip of this part of the island. The very bottom of Long Beach Island is the property of the Edwin B. Forsythe National Wildlife Refuge. Called the Holgate Unit, this wide stretch of beach is good for birdwatching, beach strolling, and surfing—but not bicycling. The reason? There are no roads or pathways, just sand. The Wildlife Refuge is, nonetheless, worth spending some time in, even if it's for a walk along the beach. Just don't plan on taking your bike with you.

The South Loop tour begins in Ship Bottom at the intersection of Central Avenue and West 9th Street. Proceed down Central Avenue to West 28th Street, where you must make a left. Ride up to the intersection with Long Beach Boulevard and turn right. Proceed down the boulevard, which runs the length of the island, to Beach Haven. Along the way you'll pass stores that sell beach paraphernalia and nautical nicknacks, surf shops and boutiques that cater to the summer tourist.

It is a good four or five miles to Beach Haven, South Long Beach Island's most popular tourist town. Once you get into Beach Haven,

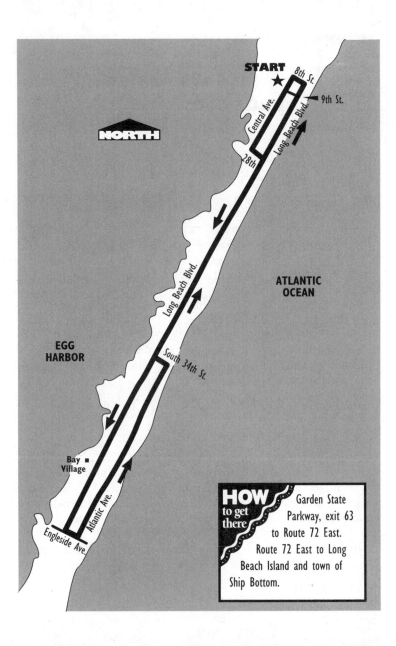

Long Beach Island South Loop: Directions at a Glance

1. South onto Central Avenue in Ship Bottom to West 28th Street.
2. Left onto West 28th Street.
3. Right onto Long Beach Boulevard.
4. Left onto Engleside Avenue in Beach Haven.
5. Left onto Atlantic Avenue.
6. Left at the conclusion of Atlantic Avenue, onto South 34th Street.
7. Right back onto Long Beach Boulevard.
8. Left onto 8th Street in Ship Bottom.
9. Tour ends at intersection of 9th Street and Central Avenue in Ship Bottom.

you'll come across Bay Village, the island's biggest shopping mall. Nearby are many other shops and eateries, as well as a miniature golf course. Finally, there is Fantasy Island, Long Beach Island's only amusement park.

After you pass these sites, you'll come to Engleside Avenue, a main thoroughfare to the beach, just a couple of blocks away. Make a left onto Engleside. You are now in Beach Haven's historic district. Although the resort doesn't have the reputation or charm of either Cape May or Ocean Grove, Beach Haven does have its share of interesting Victorian summer homes, many of which have been restored.

Ride up to the Long Beach Island Historical Museum located on the corner of Engleside and Beach avenues. Here you can pick up a walking tour brochure and view the most interesting of the Victorian homes within a three- or four-block radius of the museum.

Even if you decide against the walking tour, do plan to spend some time in the museum. It is one of the better small museums in southern New Jersey. Inside the former church, now the home of the Long Beach Island Historical Society, you'll see displays that depict the island's importance as a whaling center and photos of the now infamous March 1962 storm that devastated the island and caused millions of dollars in property damage.

Directly across the street from the museum is the Surflight Theater, a popular nightspot for island vacationers. Here drama students, up-and-coming New York actors and actresses, and even veteran players from the regional theater circuit star in a full season of musicals and comedies. Across from both the theater and museum is the Beach Haven Band Shell and adjoining field, where free concerts occur weekly throughout the summer.

After your museum visit, ride one block east (toward the ocean) on Engleside Avenue to Atlantic Avenue. Make a left onto Atlantic Avenue and begin your ride back to Ship Bottom. Notice that there is a designated bicycle lane on Atlantic Avenue to get to the sand and surf.

Continue along Atlantic Avenue to its end at South 34th Street, where you'll make a left and a few blocks later, a right back onto Long Beach Boulevard. Ride north on the boulevard through Brant Beach and Ship Bottom to 8th Street in the latter town. Here, make a left and return to your starting point on 9th Street and Central Avenue, a block away.

The Pine Barrens

County:	Burlington
Number of Miles:	25
Degree of Difficulty:	Easy
Terrain:	Flat
Surface:	Good
Things to See:	Wharton State Forest, Batsto Village and the Richards' Mansion, Mullica River, Wading River, Pine Barrens forest

The Pine Barrens cover nearly one-fourth of New Jersey. Located smack in the middle of the state, this remarkable wilderness area is home to some fifty-four threatened plant species and thirty-five threatened wildlife species. Underneath this vast area of pitch pine forest, cedar swamps, marshlands, and tea-colored rivers is the Cohansey Aquifer, a huge, seventeen-trillion-gallon lake. It's possible that the lake contains some of the purest water in America.

Much of the Pine Barrens is under federal and state protection from development and land abuse. The area is sparsely settled, and the towns found in the heart of the Pines are hardly towns at all anymore. Most contain few residents—and even fewer buildings. Some are actual ghost towns. Because of the lack of people in the Pines, there are very few paved roads. Those roads are ideal for bicycle riding, though, and two-wheel touring is a great way to experience the Pine Barrens.

Begin your ride in the Batsto Village parking area, just off Route 542. Part of Wharton State Forest, Batsto Village is a nineteenth-century bog-iron community that today features a number of restored buildings including a general store, post office, gristmill, threshing

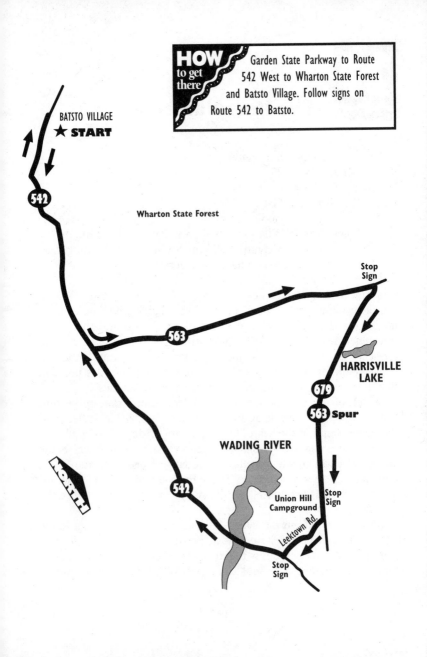

BATSTO VILLAGE
★ START

HOW to get there: Garden State Parkway to Route 542 West to Wharton State Forest and Batsto Village. Follow signs on Route 542 to Batsto.

542

Wharton State Forest

Stop Sign

563

HARRISVILLE LAKE

679
563 Spur

WADING RIVER

542

Union Hill Campground

Stop Sign

Leektown Rd.

Stop Sign

NORTH

The Pine Barrens: Directions at a Glance

1. Left onto Route 542 out of the Batsto Village parking lot.
2. Left onto Route 563.
3. Right at the intersection of Route 563 and Route 679 (also known as the Route 563 Spur and Chatsworth Road).
4. Right at the old Union Hill Campground intersection stop sign, onto Leektown Road.
5. Right at stop sign onto Route 542.
6. Route 542 to Batsto Village.

barn, workers' homes, and the Richards' Mansion, a beautiful and interesting structure once owned by bog-iron baron Jesse Richards.

Take time to stroll around Batsto Village before or after your Pine Barrens bicycle tour. Special events are frequently held at Batsto during the summer and fall. Call (609) 561–0024 for details.

Also, be certain to stop at the Visitor's Center, where you can purchase books and pamphlets about the cultural and natural history of the Pine Barrens. There are a number of fine exhibits in the Visitor's Center mini-museum; these will give you a clear picture of the importance of not only Batsto, but also the entire Pine Barrens over the past two hundred years.

Start your tour by making a left onto Route 542 and heading east. Some two miles later you'll pass a wide section of the Mullica River, one of the Pine Barrens' best canoeing rivers. Continue east on Route 542.

Make a left onto Route 563 and head north toward Chatsworth and Jenkins. The next five miles will be through Wharton State Forest. Notice the scrub pine and pitch pine trees on both sides of you. You'll pass a gun club or two but little else in the way of buildings or people. Traffic will be light, except, perhaps, on weekends and holidays.

Make a right at the intersection of Route 563 and Route 679 (also known as the Route 563 Spur). Route 679 won't be marked; look for the stop sign and turn there. Heading south now, you'll pass Harrisville Lake, Bodine Field (a major camping area in Wharton State

Forest), and more wooded area. Eventually, Route 679 will also be called Chatsworth Road.

Make a right at the old Union Hill Campground intersection onto Leektown Road. Follow signs for Batsto Village and Route 542. At the next stop sign, make a right and continue to ride to Route 542. Cross over the Wading River, another prime Pine Barrens canoeing river. You are now on Route 542 heading west. Follow it to Batsto Village, where the tour concludes.

The Lumberton–Vincentown Loop

County:	Burlington
Number of Miles:	25
Degree of Difficulty:	Easy
Terrain:	Flat
Surface:	Fair
Things to See:	Lumberton, Vincentown, South Jersey farmland, Pine Barrens

Lumberton is a small, sleepy town on the outskirts of the Pine Barrens. Located just south of Mount Holly and Rancocas State Park, Lumberton used to be a thriving river town when barges on Rancocas Creek would bring goods made in Lumberton out to the Delaware River and Philadelphia.

The Lumberton–Vincentown Loop begins in the parking lot of the Ridgeway A. Gaun Community Center on Route 541 (also called the Lumberton–Mount Holly Road), the town's main artery. The Gaun Community Center is home to the Lumberton Historical Society museum. Unfortunately its hours are quite limited, so don't expect it to be open upon your arrival. Get permission to park in the Community Center lot, or park on a side street nearby. Make a left out of the lot onto Route 541 and ride to Landing Street. Make a left onto Landing. An eighth of a mile later you'll come to a fork in the road. Stay straight. You'll now be on Municipal Drive. (If you went right at the fork, you'd stay on Landing Street.)

Proceed on Municipal Drive. You'll ride by the Lumberton Municipal Complex and police station on your right. Pass through the stop sign intersection. Municipal Drive now becomes Newbolds Corner Road. You'll now be in South Jersey countryside where sod, horse, and dairy farms sit alongside modern housing developments.

At the next stop sign, some four miles later, make a right onto

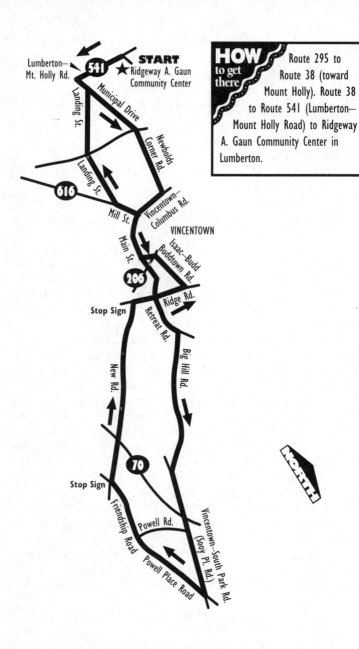

START
★ Ridgeway A. Gaun
Community Center

Lumberton—
Mt. Holly Rd.

541

Landing St.

Municipal Drive

Newbolds Corner Rd.

Landing St.

616

Mill St.

Vincentown—Columbus Rd.

VINCENTOWN

Main St.

Isaac—Budd Buddtown Rd.

206

Ridge Rd.

Stop Sign

Retreat Rd.

Big Hill Rd.

New Rd.

70

Stop Sign

Friendship Road

Powell Rd.

Powell Place Road

Vincentown—South Park Rd. (Sooy Pl. Rd.)

HOW to get there
Route 295 to Route 38 (toward Mount Holly). Route 38 to Route 541 (Lumberton—Mount Holly Road) to Ridgeway A. Gaun Community Center in Lumberton.

NORTH

The Lumberton–Vincentown Loop:
Directions at a Glance

1. Left onto Route 541, out of Ridgeway A. Gaun Community Center parking lot.
2. Left onto Landing Street.
3. At the fork, bear left. You're now on Municipal Drive. (Municipal Drive eventually becomes Newbolds Corner Road.)
4. Right onto Vincentown–Columbus Road. This road eventually becomes Main Street in Vincentown. Cross over Route 206. Main Street becomes Retreat Road.
5. At the "Y" intersection of Retreat Road and Big Hill Road, bear right onto Big Hill Road.
6. Big Hill Road turns into Vincentown–South Park Road (also called Sooy Place Road) after crossing over Route 70.
7. Right onto Powell Place Road. For shortcut, turn at Powell Road (see note on page 140 of the text). Powell Place Road eventually turns into Friendship Road.
8. Right onto New Road.
9. Right onto Ridge Road.
10. Left onto Isaac–Budd Road, known as Buddtown Road.
11. Right onto Main Street in Vincentown.
12. Left onto Mill Street.
13. Right onto Landing Street.
14. Left turn where Landing Street and Municipal Drive meet.
15. Right onto Route 541.
16. Follow Route 541 through Lumberton to Ridgeway A. Gaun Community Center.

Vincentown–Columbus Road. This road will lead you onto Main Street in Vincentown. While Lumberton has remained a quiet residential town, Vincentown is beginning to attract occasional antiques hunters and general-store lovers. In the few shops and turn-of-the-century homes, you will experience a fleeting glimpse of some of southern New Jersey's Victorian charm.

Vincentown–Columbus Road becomes Main Street in the town of Vincentown. Cross over Route 206. Main Street now becomes Retreat Road. Follow Retreat Road to the "Y" intersection. Bear right onto Big Hill Road. Follow Big Hill Road to the Route 70 intersection. On the other side of Route 70, Big Hill Road turns into Vincentown–South Park Road—according to most county maps. But the street sign at the intersections indicates the road is called Sooy Place Road.

You'll notice that the scenery on Sooy Place Road is different from the scenery outside Lumberton. You are now in the Pine Barrens. You'll pass pitch pine forest and cranberry bogs as well as recently-built small housing developments.

Continue on Sooy Place Road to the Powell Place Road intersection where the old Pine Tavern used to be (see historical marker at intersection) and a picturesque horse farm still sits. (*Note:* Before you reach Powell Place Road, you'll come to Powell Road on your right, less than a mile from Route 70. If you wish to cut a couple of miles off the tour or to avoid the sandy, gravel road surface that makes up about a half mile of Powell Place Road, turn here and ride to the intersection of Powell Road and Powell Place Road, where you'll make a right turn and proceed to New Road.) Make a right and follow Powell Place Road through the Pine Barrens town of Tabernacle. At press time a small section of Powell Place Road is unpaved, but the surface is not too difficult to traverse. Eventually, I'm told, this portion of Powell Place will be paved. Notice how development is slowly but surely creeping into the Pines. Off Powell Place Road are new side streets with new homes on them. Fifteen years ago this whole area was virgin forest.

Continue on Powell Place Road. Eventually, Powell Place Road turns into Friendship Road. At the New Road intersection and stop sign, make a right. Proceed on New Road and cross over Route 70, about a mile away. Continue on New Road to the Ridge Road intersection. There is a four-way stop sign intersection here. Make a right onto Ridge Road and proceed to Isaac–Budd Road, passing the Retreat Road stop sign intersection. Make a left onto Isaac–Budd Road, also known as Buddtown Road. You'll pass more sod and horse farms because you're now out of the Pine Barrens.

Cross over Route 206 and go to the Main Street stop sign, about a quarter mile from Route 206. Make a right onto Main Street. You're now back in Vincentown. This is the same Main Street you rode on earlier in the tour. Proceed back into the center of Vincetown, but this time make a left onto Mill Street instead of backtracking on Vincentown–Columbus Road.

A half mile from the Main Street/Mill Street intersection, make a right onto Landing Street. (If you went straight, you'd be on Route 616.)

Three miles down Landing Street you'll come to a stop sign intersection (Eayrestown Road). Pass through the intersection. Follow Landing Street to where Landing Street and Municipal Drive meet. Make a left. A quarter mile farther is the Route 541 intersection. Make a right here and ride back to the Ridgeway A. Gaun Community Center, where the tour concludes.

The Jersey Devil Run

County:	Atlantic
Number of Miles:	10.2
Degree of Difficulty:	Easy
Terrain:	Flat
Surface:	Good
Things to See:	Smithville (shops, boutiques, Tomasello Winery, Smithville Inn), Noyes Museum, Leed's Point

Located on the fringe of the Pine Barrens a few miles north of Atlantic City, the "Historic Towne of Smithville" is a popular South Jersey tourist attraction. More than thirty boutiques, shops, and restaurants comprise the town that sits on the banks of Lake Meone. Many of the buildings were constructed in the eighteenth and nineteenth centuries and were carefully moved to Smithville from other locations in the Pine Barrens. The remaining buildings in the town are colonial replicas.

The Smithville Inn, built two hundred years ago, is a popular restaurant. Back in colonial times the Baremore family catered to hungry and tired stagecoach travelers. The Inn was a working establishment until the early 1900s, when it was abandoned and fell into disrepair. In 1949, however, the Noyes family purchased the Inn and restored its original charm and usefulness. Other historic buildings were later purchased and relocated near the Smithville Inn. Gradually, merchants moved in, and Smithville began to lure tourists.

Before embarking on your tour of the Smithville–Leed's Point area, stroll through Smithville. Visit the old mill (now an antiques shop) where a large waterwheel is still capable of turning water from

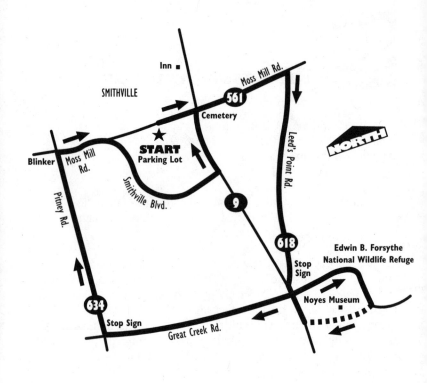

Inn ■

SMITHVILLE

Moss Mill Rd.

561

Cemetery

NORTH

Blinker

Moss Mill Rd.

★
START
Parking Lot

Smithville Blvd.

Leed's Point Rd.

Pitney Rd.

9

618

Edwin B. Forsythe
National Wildlife Refuge

Stop
Sign

Noyes Museum ■

634

Stop Sign

Great Creek Rd.

HOW
to get
there
Garden State Parkway to Route
9. Turn left onto Route 561 in
Oceanville. Smithville is located at
intersection of Routes 9 and 561.

The Jersey Devil Run: Directions at a Glance

1. Right onto Route 561 (out of the Smithville parking lot). Route 561 is also called Moss Mill Road.
2. Cross over Route 9.
3. Right onto Leed's Point Road (Route 618).
4. Left onto Route 9.
5. Left onto Great Creek Road.
6. Right onto Noyes Museum dirt road.
7. Right onto Route 9.
8. Left onto Great Creek Road.
9. Right onto Pitney Road (Route 634).
10. Right onto Moss Mill Road (Route 561).
11. Moss Mill Road becomes Smithville Boulevard. Left at Smithville Boulevard/Route 9 intersection.
12. Left at Route 9/Route 561 intersection to Smithville parking lot.

Lake Meone. If you're a wine lover, pay a visit to the Tomasello Winery, where you'll be able to sample some nineteen wines and seven champagnes, all made with grapes grown in New Jersey vineyards. Also on display are pieces of antique wine-making equipment. Other shops sell antique reproduction furniture, clothes, colonial bric-a-brac, and Pine Barrens folk art. Perhaps make lunch or dinner reservations at the Smithville Inn before you set out on the bike tour.

The tour begins in the Smithville parking lot located on Route 561, just across from the shops. Make a right out of the parking lot and onto Route 561. Two hundred yards later, you'll come upon a stop sign and the Route 9 intersection. Cross over Route 9 and head toward Leed's Point. Notice the old cemetery to your right. Many tombstones date back to the eighteenth century. Continue on Route 561, which is also called Moss Mill Road.

Approximately one and a half miles later, you'll come to Leed's Point Road (Route 618). Make a right here. This area is rich in New

Jersey folklore. According to legend, this is where the infamous Jersey Devil was born.

The way some locals tell it, the horned, winged creature, with the face of a horse and the tail of a demon, was the result of an illicit affair between a certain Mrs. Leeds and a young, handsome British army officer around the time of the Revolutionary War. Others swear a curse fell upon the thirteenth child of poor Mrs. Leeds. In any event, shortly after his birth the creature flew out an open window and has terrified the countryside ever since . . . or so legend has it.

Continue south on Route 618 until the stop sign at the Route 9 intersection. Make a left onto Route 9. Proceed for not more than a fifth of a mile, at which point you'll come to the Great Creek Road intersection. Make a left onto Great Creek Road and follow signs for the Edwin B. Forsythe National Wildlife Refuge, formerly called the Brigantine National Wildlife Refuge.

For those who would like to combine the Edwin B. Forsythe National Wildlife Refuge Tour (see page 149) with this tour, continue to the entrance of the refuge. If, however, you prefer to bicycle the wildlife refuge's dirt road loop at another time, turn right off Great Creek Road and onto the dirt road where the Noyes Museum is located. There will be a sign that identifies the dirt road and an entrance to the Noyes Museum property just after the bend in Great Creek Road. Proceed approximately two hundred yards up the dirt road. On your right will be the museum. Across from the museum is the parking lot.

The same family that purchased and restored the Smithville Inn also financed the construction of this fine arts museum. Opened in 1983, the Noyes Museum is now southern New Jersey's largest art museum, and a visit to it is highly recommended. Of particular interest is the museum's collection of waterfowl and shorebird decoys. Fred Noyes was once a serious collector of such decoys. Many of his most prized decoys are now on exhibit in the museum.

The museum also has other exhibits on display. They often feature the work of noted New Jersey sculptors, painters, and furniture makers. The museum, however, is not open every day. For information on when it is open, as well as information on current exhibits and special programs, call (609) 652–8848.

Make a left out of the Noyes Museum parking lot and go in the opposite direction from which you came. At the stop sign, which is the Route 9 intersection, make a right and proceed to Great Creek Road, approximately one-tenth of a mile north. Make a left onto Great Creek Road. (If you went right, you'd head back toward the Edwin B. Forsythe National Wildlife Refuge and the entrance to the Noyes Museum.)

Continue on Great Creek Road. It is a long stretch of road, flat and smooth, and perfect for hitting an "energetic" riding pace. At the next stop sign, make a right onto Pitney Road (Route 634). Proceed to the blinking light, which is the intersection of Pitney Road and Moss Mill Road (Route 561), and make a right. Look for Smithville Boulevard once you enter the large development complex and take it to the Route 9 intersection. Follow Smithville Boulevard to the stop sign intersection. Smithville Boulevard meets Route 9 here. Make a left onto Route 9. A mile or so down Route 9, you'll come to the Route 561 intersection. Make a left here and ride to the Smithville parking lot where the tour originates.

27 Edwin B. Forsythe
National Wildlife Refuge

County:	Atlantic
Number of Miles:	8.5
Degree of Difficulty:	Moderate
Terrain:	Flat
Surface:	Rough (dirt road)
Things to See:	Visitor's Center, Wildlife Refuge, Atlantic City skyline, marshland, Great Bay, Reed's Bay, birds

Talk about birds! More than 250 species of them visit the Edwin B. Forsythe National Wildlife Refuge, formerly the Brigantine National Wildlife Refuge, each year. You don't have to be an avid bird-watcher to appreciate this beautiful bird refuge. There are birds near the water, on the water, in the marshland, and in the sky above the Refuge. They squeak, squawk, and sing. Such sights and sounds make this tour a truly special one.

But there is a catch. The eight-and-a-half-mile Refuge loop road is not paved. It is kept in good condition by rangers, but it is a dirt road. Thus, an all-terrain or mountain bike is recommended for this tour. That is not to say, however, one couldn't complete the tour on a standard ten-speed or even a three-speed. It has been done. But riding one of these bikes will mean a rough ride, and the tour certainly won't be as enjoyable for you as it would be for those pedalling bikes equipped with fat tires.

Most people who visit the Edwin B. Forsythe National Wildlife Refuge do so by car. In fact, at the Visitor's Center a self-guided "Auto Tour" of the refuge is available. Pick up one of these pamphlets and use it as any driver would. While the pamphlet is free, there is a nominal fee to ride the Refuge loop road.

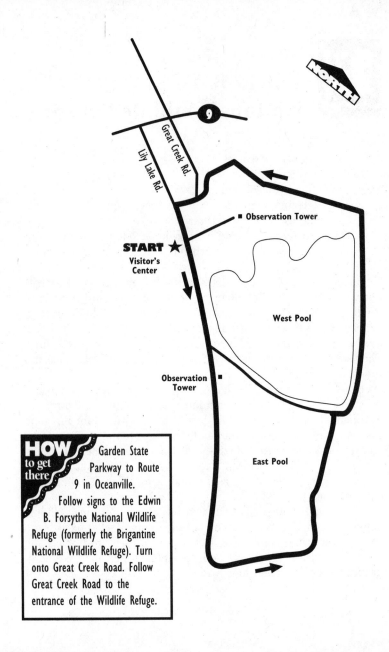

NORTH

9

Great Creek Rd.

Lily Lake Rd.

■ Observation Tower

START ★

Visitor's Center

West Pool

Observation Tower ■

HOW to get there — Garden State Parkway to Route 9 in Oceanville. Follow signs to the Edwin B. Forsythe National Wildlife Refuge (formerly the Brigantine National Wildlife Refuge). Turn onto Great Creek Road. Follow Great Creek Road to the entrance of the Wildlife Refuge.

East Pool

Edwin B. Forsythe National Wildlife Refuge: Directions at a Glance

1. Follow the dirt road loop around the Refuge.
2. At its conclusion, make a left onto Great Creek Road and ride back to the Visitor's Center parking area.

Be sure to spend some time at the Visitor's Center before you embark on your bike tour. The wildlife exhibits are informative, and the many different slide shows that rangers show in the auditorium are especially interesting. Also, pick up another pamphlet called "Birds of Edwin B. Forsythe National Wildlife Refuge." It contains a bird checklist so you can keep track of your personal sightings, if you desire. It also contains information on what season you're most apt to see what bird, plus the average number of yearly sightings. Having this kind of information at your disposal only makes the tour more rewarding.

Begin your tour at the entrance of the dirt road loop. The only directions you need are to follow the loop. The unpaved road, however, will ultimately end in a location other than where you began. You will notice that the dirt road ends on Great Creek Road—the road you took to get to the Refuge. Simply turn left onto Great Creek Road and ride back to the Visitor's Center, where you began your tour and probably parked your car. The distance is not more than a mile.

While on the loop road, you'll notice that there are fourteen numbered "stops." These correspond to information contained in the "Auto Tour" brochure. Serious bird-watcher/bicyclists can easily spend a morning or afternoon admiring the birds and beauty of the Refuge. Binoculars are recommended, but they are not mandatory to enjoy your outing. Insect repellent, however, is a good idea. Mosquitos and greenhead flies can be a nuisance.

On the loop road you'll get a superb view of the Atlantic City skyline to the south. The body of water that separates Atlantic City and the Refuge is Reed's Bay. The bay on the northern side of the Refuge is known as Great Bay.

Like most of the Jersey Shore marshland and protected natural area tours included in this book, the Edwin B. Forsythe National Wildlife Refuge is located on the Atlantic Flyway. Because of the Refuge's location, a large variety and number of birds use it as a migratory stop-off. The best time to bike the loop road and view the birds is during autumn when many birds are migrating south. Dawn and dusk are better than late morning and afternoon because birds are most active then. Those most interested in ducks and geese will want to bicycle the route in November. It will be a bit chilly perhaps, but the thousands of ducks and Canada geese that pack the refuge that month make this small discomfort worthwhile.

Cape May Point Pedal

County:	Cape May
Number of Miles:	9
Degree of Difficulty:	Easy
Terrain:	Flat
Surface:	Good
Things to See:	Cape May Bird Refuge, Sunset Beach, USS *Atlantus*, Cape May Point (town), Cape May Point State Park (lighthouse, Visitor's Center, Hawkwatch Observation Deck)

The Cape May area has more than Victorian charm to lure bicyclists and other tourists. On the outskirts of the town, and in Cape May Point, there is much to see and do. The ideal way to explore the Cape May area by bike is to make it a two-day affair. Leisurely tour the town one day, then the next day complete this tour. Setting up your bicycle exploration of Cape May and its surroundings this way will allow you to spend ample time visiting the sights along the road, rather than simply riding by them. Cape May is really too special a place to try to see it all in one day.

If you decide on a two-day outing, consider staying in one of Cape May's many excellent bed & breakfasts. Advance reservations are almost always a must. Some B&Bs even have bikes for guests' use. Cape May attracts tourists nine months of the year. Only in January, February, and March is the town not full of tourists. Unfortunately, these months aren't exactly optimum bicycling months in the Garden State.

The best time to tour Cape May is the fall. September is an excellent month, because the weather is usually warm, not hot, and the summer crowds are gone. October is a good month, too, because Cape May hosts its popular Victorian Week then. There are many

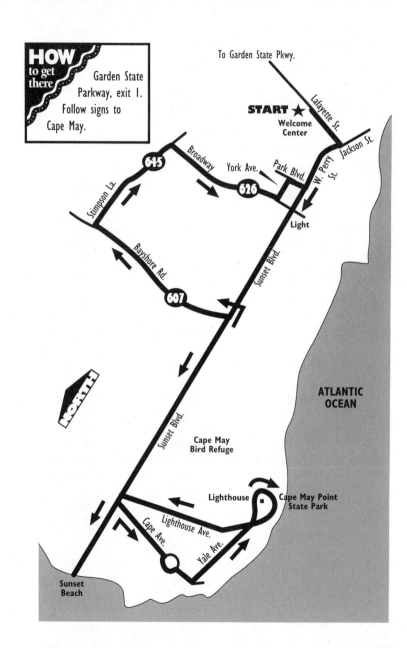

HOW to get there
Garden State Parkway, exit 1. Follow signs to Cape May.

To Garden State Pkwy.

Lafayette St.

START ★
Welcome Center

Jackson St.

645

Broadway

York Ave.

Park Blvd.

626

W. Perry St.

Stimpson La.

Light

Bayshore Rd.

607

Sunset Blvd.

NORTH

Sunset Blvd.

Cape May Bird Refuge

ATLANTIC OCEAN

Lighthouse

Cape May Point State Park

Lighthouse Ave.

Cape Ave.

Yale Ave.

Sunset Beach

Cape May Point Pedal: Directions at a Glance

1. Right onto Lafayette Street (out of the Welcome Center parking lot).
2. Right at the Jackson Street/Perry Street stop sign. Bear left onto West Perry Street.
3. West Perry Street becomes Sunset Boulevard. Ride down Sunset Boulevard to Sunset Beach.
4. Return on Sunset Boulevard to Cape Avenue. Make a right.
5. Proceed around Cape May Point circle and continue on Cape Avenue to Yale Avenue.
6. Left onto Yale Avenue.
7. Enter Cape May Point State Park.
8. Follow park road to lighthouse, Visitor's Center, and Hawkwatch Observation Deck.
9. Exit Cape May Point State Park. Make a right onto Lighthouse Avenue.
10. Right onto Sunset Boulevard.
11. Left onto Bayshore Road (Route 607).
12. Right onto Route 645 (Stimpson Lane).
13. Right onto Route 626 (Broadway).
14. Left onto York Avenue.
15. Right onto Park Boulevard.
16. Left onto West Perry Street.
17. Left onto Lafayette Street.
18. Left into the Welcome Center parking lot.

special events to enjoy, including house tours, antiques and craft shows, and square dancing contests.The streets are congested, however, especially on weekends, which doesn't make for ideal cycling situations. If you do go to Cape May to bicycle during Victorian Week, make it on a weekday, if possible. That way your cycling experience should be a rewarding one, since there will be fewer cars on the roads.

The Cape May Point Pedal begins in the Welcome Center parking lot on Lafayette Street in Cape May. Make a right out of the parking lot onto Lafayette Street. Approximately fifty yards down the road is a stop sign. To the left of the sign is Jackson Street; to the right is Perry Street. Make a right at the stop sign and proceed to the next intersection, which comes up quickly. Bear left here to stay on Perry Street. Swain's Hardware store will be on your right. The brightly painted Bernard-Goode House, a popular bed & breakfast with the best breakfast spread in town, will be on your left.

Perry Street becomes West Perry Street after you pass Swain's Hardware store. Then, once you're beyond the traffic light at the intersection of West Perry and Broadway, West Perry becomes Sunset Boulevard. Head down Sunset. Your destination is Sunset Beach, which is located at the end of Sunset Boulevard, some two miles away.

Along the way you'll pass the Cape May Bird Refuge. Those cyclists interested in bird-watching will find a stop here worthwhile. If you are a bird-watcher, do pack binoculars. You'll get a chance to use them here and then again in Cape May Point State Park.

Once you arrive at Sunset Beach, find a suitable bicycle parking space and walk to the water. Offshore a few hundred yards you'll notice what looks like a concrete bulkhead. Actually, it the remains of the USS *Atlantus,* a 3,000-ton concrete freighter built in the waning days of World War I when steel was scarce. The concrete ship experiment was a failure due to the excessive weight and density of such a vessel. In 1926 the *Atlantus* went aground during a storm. Now it's a state historic site.

Sunset Beach is interesting for another reason, too. It is where you can find "Cape May diamonds," quartz crystals that bear a remarkable resemblance to real diamonds. Don't fret if you can't find one; you can purchase all you want in the shops that line the Sunset Beach parking lot.

After visiting Sunset Beach, backtrack on Sunset Boulevard until you come to Cape Avenue and the columned entrance to Cape May Point. Make a right onto Cape Avenue and head toward Cape May Point State Park, your next destination.

A few blocks down Cape Avenue is a circle. Bear right around it until you meet up with Cape Avenue again (it is halfway around the circle). Proceed down Cape Avenue until the intersection with Yale Avenue. Make a left here. Pass the Cape May Point Post Office on your right. Continue on Yale Avenue to the intersection of Lehigh Avenue. Across from the intersection is the entrance to Cape May Point State Park.

Proceed into the park. On your right is the Cape May Point Lighthouse. Just beyond the lighthouse, bear right and proceed to the Visitor's Center. You'll want to spend some time here. Check out the nature exhibits and familiarize yourself with park activities by way of the many free pamphlets available. You might also want to visit the lighthouse. There is, however, an entrance fee to enter the lighthouse interior and climb the steps to the top.

Across from the Visitor's Center is the Hawkwatch Observation Deck. Pedal over and check out the latest hawk sighting tally. Once again, bird-watchers might want to spend a bit more time here than non-birders.

Follow the exit signs and leave the park the same way you rode in. At the stop sign make a right onto Lighthouse Avenue. Proceed on Lighthouse Avenue to Sunset Boulevard. Make a right onto Sunset and head back toward Cape May. Pass the Cape May Bird Refuge again, but instead of continuing on Sunset Boulevard, make a left onto Bayshore Road (Route 607).

Proceed on Bayshore Road, a particularly scenic country road, to Route 645 (Stimpson Lane). Make a right onto Route 645 and ride to the intersection/stop sign. Make a right onto Route 626. Eventually, Route 626 becomes Broadway. Continue on Broadway to York Avenue. Make a left onto York and go to the Park Boulevard intersection. Make a right onto Park. At the Myrtle Street stop sign, carefully make your second left onto West Perry St. (Myrtle Street is a one-way road.) Continue on West Perry Street and follow the Parkway signs. At the West Perry/Lafayette Street intersection, make a left. Just up on your left is the Welcome Center, your starting and ending point.

Cape May
Court House Hop

County:	Cape May
Number of Miles:	11.5
Degree of Difficulty:	Easy
Terrain:	Flat
Surface:	Good
Things to See:	Cape May Museum, Cape May County Park and Zoo, Cape May Court House

Too often historic Cape May Court House is overlooked by vacationers and bicyclists eager to get to Cape May, one of the south Jersey Shore's prime destinations. Cape May Court House is less of a tourist town than its sister community. It still has a warm, small-town character that reminds one of New England, which, by the way, is where the area's first settlers came from in the seventeenth century. Cape May Court House also has a number of historic buildings dating back more than two hundred years, making the town a great starting point for a tour of the Cape May peninsula's central region.

The tour begins in the parking lot of the Cape May County Museum, which is located on Route 9, less than a mile from exit 11 on the Garden State Parkway. Before getting on your bicycle, spend some time in the museum, one of the best on the south Jersey Shore. Run by the Cape May County Historical and Genealogical Society, the museum is housed in the John Holmes House, a pre–Revolutionary War structure.

Among the many items on display in the museum are pieces of furniture dating as far back as the late seventeenth century, surgical instruments from the American Revolution up to the Spanish American War as well as other military memorabilia, and various historical

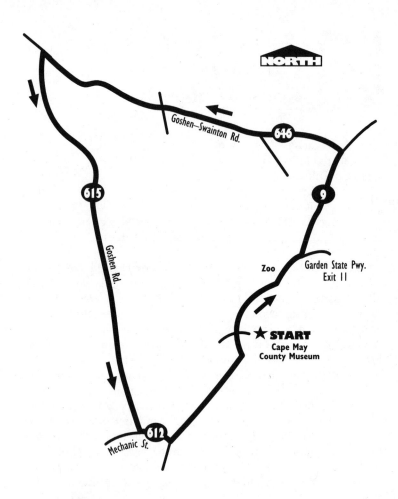

NORTH

Goshen–Swainton Rd.

646

615

9

Goshen Rd.

Zoo

Garden State Pwy.
Exit 11

★ **START**
Cape May
County Museum

612

Mechanic St.

HOW to get there — Garden State Parkway to exit 11. Route 609 (Crest Haven Road) to Route 9. Left on Route 9. The Cape May County Museum (John Holmes House) is about two hundred yards down the road on the left.

Cape May Court House Hop: Directions at a Glance

1. Right out of Cape May Museum Gift Shop parking lot onto Route 9.
2. Left into Cape May County Park and Zoo.
3. After touring zoo, exit park. Left onto Route 9 north.
4. Bear left at stop sign intersection and continue on Route 9 north.
5. Left at Route 646 intersection (Goshen–Swainton Road); head west on Route 646.
6. Left onto Route 615 (Goshen Road).
7. Left onto Route 612 (Mechanic Street).
8. Left onto Route 9.
9. Right into Cape May Museum Gift Shop parking lot.

documents that help tell the story of Cape May from its earliest days as a whaling settlement to the present. The museum also has an eighteenth-century kitchen and bedroom stocked with period pieces and artifacts, and a furnished Victorian room. In the barn outside you'll find a duck decoy collection, old whaling tools, the Cape May Lighthouse lens, and various antique wagons. Guided tours are available. There is a nominal admission charge to the museum. Call for museum hours (609–465–3535).

Once you've toured the Cape May County Museum, it's time to mount your bicycle and begin the tour of Cape May Court House and its environs. Exit the museum parking lot and make a right onto Route 9. Although this is a busy roadway, it has wide, well-paved shoulders that will keep you out of the auto traffic.

Your first stop, the Cape May County Park and Zoo, is less than a mile from the museum parking lot. Make a left into the park entrance and proceed to the zoo, one of the best-kept secrets of the south Jersey Shore. You might think that a county zoo can't be anything more than a small petting zoo that caters to young children. Not here in Cape May. With monkeys, tigers, zebras, bears, exotic birds, lions, oryx, giraffes, and various reptiles, the Cape May County Zoo is at least as good as any zoo found elsewhere in New Jersey, and it's free.

Of course you can't ride your bike through the zoo, so you'll have to park it and lock it outside the zoo entrance. It is possible to walk through the zoo in less than an hour, but you could spend half a day observing the animals. Afterwards, you might also want to spend time riding the roads in the park before returning to the entrance/exit on Route 9 and continuing your tour of Cape May Court House.

Upon exiting the park, make a left back onto Route 9, heading north. Approximately a mile up the road, you'll come to a stop sign intersection. Do not bear right or you'll find yourself on the Garden State Parkway, where bicycles are forbidden and cars whiz by at sixty miles per hour. Instead, bear left and remain on Route 9. As you continue riding north, you'll pass an occasional antiques shop—Route 9 is often referred to as "Antique Alley." On your right you'll also pass the Avalon Country Club.

Make a left turn at the Route 646 intersection (Goshen–Swainton Road) and head toward Goshen. You are now riding west. Although the shoulder on Route 646 is not as wide as that on Route 9, this road isn't quite as busy. Continue through the Route 652 intersection and pass the Big Timber Camping Resort on your right.

Pass through a second intersection, where Route 657 and Route 646 cross. About two hundred yards down the road, you'll ride over abandoned railroad tracks and leave the residential area you've just ridden through. Now the setting gets more rural and scenic. You'll pass Green Holly Campground on your left. Eventually you'll come to the Route 615 (Goshen Road) intersection, where you'll make a left and head south toward the town of Cape May Court House. You'll pass a wildlife refuge on your left; to your right a few miles west is Delaware Bay.

When you arrive at the Route 615/Route 612 (Mechanic Street) stop sign intersection a couple of miles down the road, make a left and proceed into the town of Cape May Court House. Notice the historic houses on Route 612. On this street are also a couple of small eateries where you might want to stop for lunch. At the Route 9 traffic light, not a mile from where you turned onto Route 612, make a left. On your right you'll see more historic homes and county government buildings. (Cape May Court House is Cape May's county seat.)

Proceed north on Route 9; once again be aware of the traffic. Pass through the Route 657 intersection and continue north on Route 9. Beyond this intersection the shoulder becomes significantly wider. Continue pedalling north on Route 9 until you come to the entrance of the Cape May County Museum parking lot, the starting point of this tour.

Belleplain State Forest Loop

County:	Cape May
Number of Miles:	20.1
Degree of Difficulty:	Easy
Terrain:	Flat
Surface:	Good
Things to See:	Belleplain State Forest and environs

Located in upper Cape May County, Belleplain State Forest is a sprawling 11,000-acre preserve of pine and other indigenous trees that shows natural New Jersey at its best. During the spring, summer, and fall, Belleplain State Forest hosts campers from all over New Jersey, as well as from New York, Pennsylvania, Delaware, and other nearby states.

With its two hundred tent sites spread over one hundred acres, Belleplain is one of southern New Jersey's largest camping destinations (call 609–861–2404 for camping information and reservations). Many vacationers come to Belleplain to hike, bird-watch, and canoe on Lake Nummy (named for a Leni-Lenape Indian chief). Others come to Belleplain for its close proximity to such south Jersey Shore vacation spots as Wildwood and Sea Isle City.

For you, the bicyclist, setting up camp at Belleplain offers all of the above advantages as well as an additional one: From Belleplain you can explore on two wheels a good portion of upper Cape May, where roads are generally excellent and both Delaware Bay and the Atlantic Ocean are within an hour's ride on a good day.

This tour begins in the parking lot of the Belleplain Visitor's Center, where camping permits are issued. Make a right out of the parking lot onto Route 550 and head toward Dennisville. A little more than a

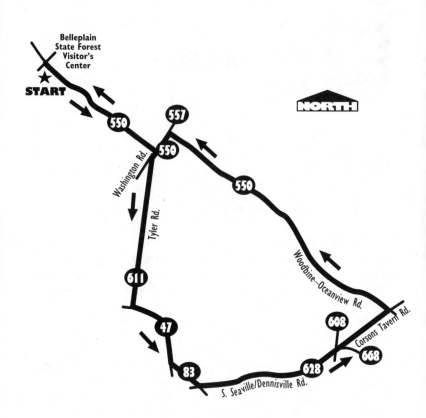

Belleplain State Forest Visitor's Center

START

550

557

550

550

Washington Rd.

Tyler Rd.

Woodbine—Oceanview Rd.

611

47

608

Corsons Tavern Rd.

668

83

628

S. Seaville/Dennisville Rd.

NORTH

HOW to get there Garden State Parkway to exit 17. Follow signs to Route 9. Right on Route 9. Left on Route 550 to Belleplain State Forest Visitor's Center parking lot.

Belleplain State Forest Loop: Directions at a Glance

1. Right out of the Belleplain State Forest Visitor's Center parking lot onto Route 550.
2. Right onto Route 557.
3. Bear left onto Route 611 (Tyler Road).
4. Left onto Route 47.
5. Left onto Route 83 (to Clermont, Avalon, Sea Isle City).
6. Left onto Route 628 (South Seaville Road, which becomes Dennisville Road, and then Corsons Tavern Road after the Route 608/Route 668 intersection).
7. Left onto Route 550 (Woodbine–Oceanview Road).
8. Left onto Route 557 (Washington Avenue).
9. Right onto Route 550 (Belleplain–Woodbine Road).
10. Left into the Belleplain State Forest Visitor's Center parking lot.

mile down the road you'll come to the stop sign intersection of Routes 550 and 557. Make a right onto Route 557. About one hundred yards beyond this intersection, bear left onto Route 611 (Tyler Road).

Three miles down Route 611 you'll come to a traffic light and a "T" intersection. Make a left onto Route 47, heading south. This is a major thoroughfare, so traffic can get heavy, especially on weekends and holidays. Fortunately, the shoulder is wide enough so you can ride safely on the road. Look for an old cemetery on your right and branch of the Dennis Creek on your left. Continue south on Route 47; on your right you'll pass protected wetlands, an indication that Delaware Bay is not far off to your west.

Make a left at the Route 83 intersection and head toward Clermont, Avalon, and Sea Isle City. Route 83, like Route 47, is a main highway, but it has little or no shoulder. The good news is that you're on Route 83 for only a short stretch before you make a left onto Route 628, also known as South Seaville Road, and ride north. About a mile up the road, South Seaville Road turns into Dennisville Road.

Eventually you'll enter the village of Seaville. You'll pass the South

Seaville Camp Meeting on your left just before you come upon the intersection of Routes 628, 668, and 608. Pass through the intersection and continue on Route 628. At this point Route 628, which is also called Dennisville Road, becomes Corsons Tavern Road. When you come to the Route 550 intersection, make a left. Route 550 is also called Woodbine–Oceanview Road. Proceed through the Route 610 intersection and follow signs back to Belleplain State Forest. The terrain here is flat and wooded, with some farms and developments. A good landmark to look for is the Woodbine Airport on your left.

Eventually you'll come to the Route 557 stop sign intersection. Make a left onto Route 557, which doubles as Route 550. To add to the confusion, Route 557/Route 550 is also called Washington Avenue. A half mile down the road Route 557 continues straight, while Route 550 goes right. Turn right onto Route 550, heading west toward the Belleplain State Forest Visitor's Center parking lot, your final destination.

Cumberland County Conquest

County:	Cumberland
Number of Miles:	23.3
Degree of Difficulty:	Moderate
Terrain:	Some hills
Surface:	Good
Things to See:	Bridgeton historic district, Cumberland County farmland

The city of Bridgeton might not be a major tourist attraction in New Jersey, due, in part, to its rather remote setting in the southwest corner of the state. Yet it contains the largest historic district in New Jersey, with a number of museums and architecturally interesting homes to visit, some of which date back to the eighteenth century.

Settled in the late 1600s, Bridgeton eventually became a southern New Jersey industrial center and a commercial hub for many Cumberland County farmers and tradesmen. Today Bridgeton, like many New Jersey cities, has sections that sorely need a facelift. But if history is a passion of yours, a day spent visiting the Bridgeton landmarks before embarking on your tour of Cumberland County farmland should prove rewarding.

The Bridgeton–Cumberland Tourist Association publishes a free pamphlet called "A Walking Tour of Historic Bridgeton," which can be obtained by contacting the Association's office at (609) 451–4802. You can also visit the Association's headquarters in person, since this tour begins and ends in the Bridgeton Tourist Center parking lot at the intersection of Routes 49 and 77 in Bridgeton.

In addition to requesting the Walking Tour pamphlet, ask the tourist representative for information on Potter's Tavern, a restored

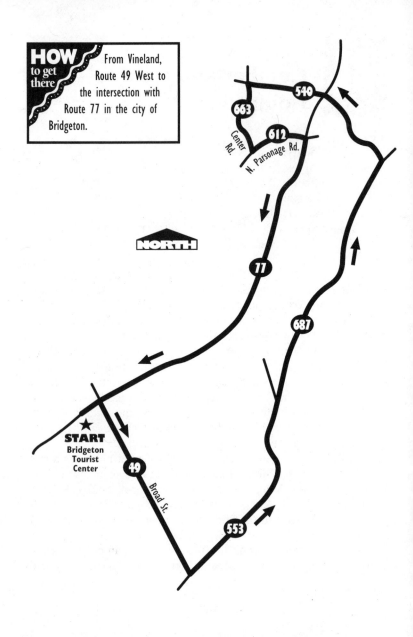

HOW to get there — From Vineland, Route 49 West to the intersection with Route 77 in the city of Bridgeton.

663

540

612

Center Rd.

N. Parsonage Rd.

NORTH

71

687

★ **START**
Bridgeton Tourist Center

49

Broad St.

553

Cumberland County Conquest:
Directions at a Glance

1. Right out of the parking lot of the Bridgeton Tourist Center onto Route 49 (Broad Street).
2. Left onto Route 553.
3. Bear right onto Route 687.
4. Left onto Route 540.
5. Left onto Route 663 (Center Road).
6. Left onto Route 612 (North Parsonage Road).
7. Right onto Route 77.
8. At intersection of Routes 77 and 49, return to the Bridgeton Tourist Center parking lot.

---

eighteenth-century landmark and home of New Jersey's first newspaper, *The Plain Dealer.* You might also ask for information on the seventeenth-century-styled New Sweden Farmstead Museum, which tells the story of early Swedish colonists in southern New Jersey, and the George Woodruff Indian Museum, which contains more than 20,000 artifacts related to the Leni-Lenape Indians.

When you're finished exploring Bridgeton, begin your bike tour of the Cumberland County countryside, some of the prettiest in all of New Jersey. Make a right out of the Bridgeton Tourist Center parking lot onto Route 49, heading east. Route 49 is also called Broad Street within the city limits of Bridgeton.

Stay on Route 49; you'll pass the Cumberland County library office and county garages. Eventually you'll arrive at the Route 49/Route 553 intersection. Make a left onto Route 553, heading toward Woodruff. You'll notice that Bridgeton's urban environment quickly gives way to a more rural setting. Route 553 is a country road bordered by farmland. Go through the Route 552 and Route 659 stop sign intersections, remaining on Route 553. The next major intersection you come to is where Route 553 crosses Route 56. There is a traffic light here; continue on Route 553 until the intersection with

Route 687. Bear right onto Route 687 and continue on this country road until you come to a major intersection, this one with Route 540. Make a left onto Route 540 and head west, passing through more scenic Cumberland County farmland. Pass through the Route 540/Route 77 intersection, heading toward Cohansey. Make a left at the intersection with Route 663, which is also called Center Road. You're now heading south.

Go through the first stop sign intersection on Center Road. At the second stop sign, which is about three hundred yards from the first and located at the "T" intersection, make a left turn onto Route 612. A quarter mile down the road, you'll come to a "Y" intersection; bear left. You'll still be on Route 612, although here it's called North Parsonage Road. Continue on Route 612 until it intersects with Route 77. Make a right onto Route 77 and head back into Bridgeton, passing through part of the commercial section of the city. Continue on Route 77 until it intersects with Route 49, at the tour's starting point.

Salem County Sweep

County:	Salem
Number of Miles:	28.2
Degree of Difficulty:	Moderate
Surface:	Good
Things to See:	Historic Salem, Salem County countryside

Like Bridgeton, the town of Salem is full of New Jersey history that extends all the way back to the earliest days of European settlement in the state. Salem was founded by Quakers in 1675; they named their village after the Hebrew word for peace, *shalom*. Before the Quakers arrived, Dutch, Swedish, and Finnish farmers tried unsuccessfully to settle the area.

There are plenty of historic buildings in the vicinity of this tour's starting and finishing point at the Martin Luther King Memorial Park Bandshell on Route 45 (Market Street). The old Salem Courthouse dates back to 1735; the Alexander Grant House, built in 1721, is the current home of the Salem County Historical Society's museum. The Salem Friends Meetinghouse (1772) and the Robert Gibbon Johnson House (1806) are also worth visiting, as are the First United Methodist Church (1888) and the First Baptist Church (1846). All of these historic buildings are within walking distance of each other. For more information on them and on Salem's other historical points of interest, contact the Salem County Historical Society (609–935–5004) or the Greater Salem County Chamber of Commerce (609–935–1415).

Begin your bike tour of the surrounding countryside after you've had a chance to soak up some of the local history. As stated above, the tour begins in the parking lot of the Martin Luther King Memorial Park Bandshell on Route 45 (Market Street), across from the Historic Information Center and the Greater Salem Chamber of

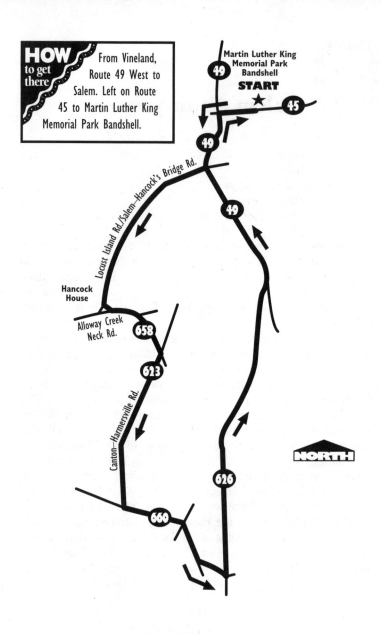

HOW to get there — From Vineland, Route 49 West to Salem. Left on Route 45 to Martin Luther King Memorial Park Bandshell.

Martin Luther King Memorial Park Bandshell
START

49

45

49

49

Locust Island Rd./Salem–Hancock's Bridge Rd.

Hancock House

Alloway Creek Neck Rd.

658

623

Canton–Harmersville Rd.

626

660

NORTH

Salem County Sweep: Directions at a Glance

1. Begin tour at Martin Luther King Memorial Park Bandshell on Route 45 (Market Street). Right out of parking lot onto Route 45.
2. Left on Route 49.
3. Right on Locust Island Road (also called Salem–Hancock's Bridge Road).
4. Left on Alloway Creek Neck Road.
5. Bear right onto Route 658.
6. Right onto Route 623 (Canton–Harmersville Road).
7. Left onto Route 660.
8. Hard left onto Route 626.
9. Left onto Route 49.
10. Right onto Route 45 to Martin Luther King Memorial Park Bandshell.

Commerce Building. Make a right out of the Bandshell lot onto Route 45 and go to the Route 49 intersection a few hundred yards away, where you'll turn left. Head east on Route 49 until the intersection with Locust Island Road, also known as Salem–Hancock's Bridge Road. A sign there points the way to Hancocks Bridge and the Hancock House, yet another historic Salem building. Make a right onto Locust Island Road, following signs to the Hancock House.

After you've visited the Hancock House, continue on Locust Island Road until the intersection with Alloway Creek Neck Road. Make a left here and head toward Canton. An eighth of a mile down the road, you'll come to a "Y" intersection. Bear right onto Route 658 (Hancock's Bridge–Harmersville Road) heading toward Canton and Greenwich. At the intersection with Route 623 South (Canton–Harmersville Road), go right.

Ride on Route 623 until you come to Route 660. Make a left turn onto Route 660. Notice the picturesque New Jersey farmland scenery. The slightly rolling hills make for excellent cycling. At the intersection that has a sign indicating ROADTOWN, SHILOH, BRIDGETON straight ahead, bear to your left. A quarter mile up the road you'll come to the Route 626 intersection. Make a hard left. Route 626 will lead you into Cumberland County. Notice the difference in terrain. Instead of farmland on both sides of the road, there is scrub forest.

Continue riding on Route 626; a few miles up the road you'll reenter Salem County. Ultimately, you'll come to the Route 49 intersection. Turn left here, heading back to the town of Salem. At the next traffic light, you'll see a historical marker by Quinton's Bridge. A Revolutionary War skirmish occurred here. Continue riding on Route 49 West until the intersection with Route 45 in the center of Salem. Make a right and ride back to the Martin Luther King Memorial Park Bandshell, where the tour began.

About the Author

Born and raised in New Jersey, travel, music, and sports writer Robert Santelli frequently contributes articles to *New Jersey Monthly, Rolling Stone, Family Circle, Surfer's Journal,* and *Caribbean Travel and Life.* A music critic and travel correspondent for the *Asbury Park Press,* he is also the author of *Guide to the Jersey Shore,* published by The Globe Pequot Press.

Short Bike Rides and Best Bike Rides

Here are the other fine titles offered in the Short Bike Rides and Best Bike Rides series, created for those who enjoy recreational cycling.

Short Bike Rides in and around Los Angeles, $11.95
Short Bike Rides in and around New York City, $9.95
Short Bike Rides in and around Philadelphia, $9.95
Short Bike Rides in and around San Francisco, $9.95
Short Bike Rides in and around Washington, D.C., $9.95
Short Bike Rides in Central and Western Massachusetts, $12.95
Short Bike Rides in Colorado, $10.95
Short Bike Rides in Connecticut, $9.95
Short Bike Rides in Eastern Massachusetts, $14.95
Short Bike Rides in Eastern Pennsylvania, $9.95
Short Bike Rides on Long Island, $8.95
Short Bike Rides in Michigan, $10.95
Short Bike Rides in Rhode Island, $10.95
Short Bike Rides in Western Washington, $12.95
Short Bike Rides on Cape Cod, Nantucket, Vineyard, $9.95

The Best Bike Rides in California, $12.95
The Best Bike Rides in New England, $12.95
The Best Bike Rides in the Mid-Atlantic, $12.95
The Best Bike Rides in the Midwest, $12.95
The Best Bike Rides in the Pacific Northwest, $12.95
The Best Bike Rides in the South, $12.95

To order any of these titles with MASTERCARD or VISA, call toll-free (800) 243-0495; fax (800) 820-2329. Free shipping for orders of three or more books. Shipping charge of $3.00 per book for one or two books ordered. Connecticut residents add sales tax. Ask for a free catalogue of Globe Pequot's quality books on travel, nature, gardening, cooking, crafts, and more. Prices and availability subject to change.